Jesus is Alive!

For Kids Evidence for the Resurrection with Gwen Ellis

Josh McDowell
Sean McDowell

EasyRead Large

Copyright Page from the Original Book

Published by Regal
From Gospel Light
Ventura, California, U.S.A.
www.regalbooks.com
Printed in the U.S.A.

Library of Congress Cataloging-in-Publication Data
McDowell, Josh.
Jesus is alive! / Josh McDowell and Sean McDowell with Gwen Ellis.
p. cm.
ISBN 978-0-8307-4786-3 (trade paper)
1. Conversion—Christianity. 2. Youth—Religious life. I. McDowell, Sean. II. Ellis, Gwen. III. Title.
BV4921.3.M34 2009
232'.5—dc22
2008046383

1 2 3 4 5 6 7 8 9 10 / 15 14 13 12 11 10 09

Set in 16 pt. Verdana

INTRODUCTION

Are Your Children Prepared for the Spiritual Challenges of this Generation?

Research reveals that our children are in a precarious position. Although many of the children who are involved in church and who are in Christian families make a profession of faith in Jesus Christ during their formative years, that decision alone does not equip them to face the spiritual challenges of their generation.

Based on our personal research and experience, we are convinced that the number one fear among Christian parents is that they will not be able to pass their values and beliefs to their children. As incredible as it may seem, research shows that "accepting Christ" and making a profession of faith today make little to no difference in a young person's attitude and behavior. You have probably seen the statistics. In one study, 74 percent of Christian teenagers said they had cheated on school tests, 83 percent said they had lied to their teachers, 93 percent said they had lied to their parents, and 63 percent said they had become physically violent toward others when angered.[1] The reality is that we lay the foundation for biblical truth when our children are very young ... long before they become teenagers.

If something is not done now, your children will probably accept the beliefs of the current teens in the church. According to the Barna Research Group, here is what our present teenagers believe:

- 65 percent don't believe Jesus is the Son of the one true God.
- 58 percent believe all faiths teach equally valued truths.
- 51 percent don't believe Jesus rose from the dead.
- 65 percent don't believe Satan is a real entity.
- 68 percent don't believe the Holy Spirit is a real entity.
- 70 percent don't believe an absolute moral truth exists.[2]

But does any of this matter? We may prefer for our children and young people to embrace biblical beliefs, but what harm will come if they don't? Research consistently shows that what a person believes translates into attitudes and behavior. The vast majority of our young people have distorted beliefs about Christ and Christianity, and the research shows that those with such distorted views are:

- 200 percent more likely to be disappointed in life
- 200 percent more likely to physically hurt someone

- 210 percent more likely to lack purpose
- 300 percent more likely to use illegal drugs
- 600 percent more likely to attempt suicide[3]

Something must be done—something different from what we are presently doing to reverse this trend. We need to teach and develop a life-changing experience within our children at a younger age. We need a fundamental change in the way Christianity is presented to our children. We need to shift from simply leading our kids to accept Christ to leading them to form an intimate relationship with him and to embracing deepened convictions about him. We need to show them how a person's beliefs are integrated into his or her lifestyle.

To raise our children to be committed followers of Christ, we must start early so that we can pass on life-changing truth to them. We must teach our children when their minds and hearts are young and pliable. If our children are not taught and modeled this truth, they will adapt to the distorted beliefs of the young people in the church of today.

King David's question, "When the foundations are being destroyed, what can the righteous do?" (Psalm 11:3), is as pertinent today as when he first asked it. *Jesus Is Alive!* has been designed for you to help teach your children about Jesus' resurrection and how that truth can affect their lives. It will help you to ground your children in what the Bible teaches about Jesus and his resurrection so that you can build a firm foundation for their spiritual future. It will help you give clear and direct answers to their questions about God, the Bible, Jesus and his resurrection.

To maximize the impact of this book in your child's life, we recommend that you first read *Evidence for the Resurrection* so that you will personally have a greater understanding and knowledge about Christ's resurrection. This will give you greater confidence to interact with your child. Next, read *Jesus Is Alive!* by yourself two or three times, and then read it aloud to your child. Be ready to reinforce the text with short, pertinent questions, and be sure to really listen to what your son or daughter has to say. Finally, share your own testimony about how you came to Christ and the difference he has made in your life.

It's easy to get discouraged and frustrated about the state of our culture. Kids are facing challenges today that we never could have imagined even a decade ago. But as difficult as parenting may be, don't lose hope. Fear is never from the Lord. Regardless of how coarse culture may become, parents are still the prime influence on the values and behaviors of children. Take the time to build a healthy relationship with your kids and intentionally teach them the biblical truths found in this book. Doing so will give them a tremendous advantage to become all God wants them to be. Go for it!

Notes

[1] "The Ethics of American Youth—2002 Report Card," conducted and published by Josephson Institute of Ethics (Marina del Rey, CA: Josephson Institute of Ethics, 2002).

[2] The Barna Research Group, "Third Millennium Teens" (Ventura, CA: The Barna Research Group, Ltd, 1999), p.51.

[3] "The Churched Youth Survey" (Dallas, TX: Josh McDowell Ministry, 1994), pp.65, 69.

Q: What event does Christmas truly celebrate, and what did the disciples believe that Jesus was born to do?

A: Many of us think that Christmas is the happiest time of the year. We love the parties, the food and, most of all, the presents that come with Christmas. But that's not all that Christmas is about. It is about the time when God gave the best present ever to all humans. That present was Jesus, his son. When Jesus was born, the shepherds heard the angels sing about God's gift. The wise men saw his star in the east and came looking for him. And the angel told Joseph to name the baby Jesus. The name Jesus means "savior," and that was what this baby was born to do: save people from their sins.

The disciples of Jesus—Peter, James, John and the rest of them—weren't there when Jesus was born. They didn't hear the angels sing. They didn't see the wise men worshiping him. They didn't really understand that he had come to save people. Instead, they believed that Jesus was the one whom God had sent to deliver them from the Romans who ruled over them and their land, and who were crushing them as a people. But they were wrong. They missed the whole point of why Jesus came to earth.

A Word from Josh and Sean

Lots of people miss the point about why Jesus was sent to earth. A long time ago, there were a handful of devout Jewish people who thought Jesus was the "Messiah," the deliverer, who would free them from the Romans and set up a permanent and truly godly kingdom on earth. They could even point to the writing of the prophet Isaiah that the Messiah would come and restore all things to a paradise where there would be no more fighting, oppression, fear or death. The disciples believed that Jesus was born to make the entire earth a pristine garden, where everyone would live together in peace forever. As we go on answering questions in this book, you'll see how wrong they were and what God's real plan for humans was and is.

"Jesus [said] ... 'For this reason I was born, and for this I came into the world, to testify to the truth'" (John 18:37).

Q: What happened to Jesus, the great hope for the future?

A: Far from freeing Israel from the Romans' rule, Jesus was executed by them. Try to imagine what you might have been thinking if you had been one of the disciples on the day Jesus died. You had believed with all your heart that Jesus had come to free you and your people from Roman rule and set up a kingdom of peace and prosperity. Now, there he was, hanging on the cross, dying. The disciples couldn't believe what was happening. Their fate hung on that cross. Their hopes for the future were being crucified. They felt what most of us would have felt: confused, sad, angry and hopeless.

The disciples believed that the man who was dying on the cross was the one whom God had promised to lead everyone out of pain and misery into a never-ending life. But now all hope was gone. Eternal life was just an empty dream. The one they had pinned their hopes on would soon be dead, and that was going to be the end of their hope of becoming free from Rome.

A Word from Josh and Sean

Too often, we think we know what is going to happen next, and when it doesn't happen the way we think, we are disappointed. The disciples felt that way. But God had a plan. God was in love with us. He could not stand the thought of losing us. He looked into the future he had planned for us. When he knew that we could never live in his presence in eternity because of sin, it broke his heart. Even though humans had rejected God, his great love could not bear the thought of us being destroyed. God wanted us back, so he thought up a solution that would save us from sin, and that solution was Jesus, hanging on a cross and dying. We're going to talk more about God's great love and Jesus' great sacrifice for us in this book. Stay with us as we go on with our questions and answers.

"Christ made a single sacrifice for sins.... It was a perfect sacrifice by a perfect person to perfect some very imperfect people. By that single offering, he did everything that needed to be done for everyone who takes part in the purifying process" (Hebrews 10:10-14, THE MESSAGE).

Q: What were the disciples feeling after Jesus' death, and what was their greatest surprise on Easter Sunday?

A: Let's pretend that you are one of the disciples, and it is Sunday morning after Jesus had been crucified. What do you think you might be feeling? Do you think you might be afraid that you would be caught and crucified too? That's what the disciples were thinking and feeling. They were afraid, and they were devastated that the one they thought would save them was dead and buried. They figured that Jesus had been the last hope for humanity. Now all hope was gone. The idea of living forever in heaven was just a dream that had gone away.

Can you see why the disciples might not have believed the women who returned from the tomb on Sunday morning and told them that Jesus' tomb was empty? Since most people never see an angel, the disciples had a hard time believing that the women had, and they really had a hard time believing what the women said the angels told them—that Jesus was alive again. But it was true, and it was the greatest surprise the world has ever seen. Dead people just don't come alive every day. So what was God up to now?

A Word from Josh and Sean

Jesus was the Messiah, and death could not keep him in the grave. God brought him back to life to fulfill his mission and bring eternal life to the world. Jesus made an amazing claim to his disciples. He said that in the future they too would have resurrected bodies like his. These would be bodies that would never age or die. They would have new life, without death or pain, in the presence of a loving God forever. When we all reach heaven, we will say, "This is what we were made for!" Remember what Jesus said just before he died: "Take heart, because I have overcome the world." It's good to remember his words when we have difficult times. No matter how bad it gets, we will one day live in heaven with Jesus—forever.

"I know that my Redeemer lives, and that in the end he will stand upon the earth" (Job 19:25).

Q: If everything God made was good, how did things get so messed up?

A: Everybody knows that when you look around, you can see that the world is a mess. There is hunger and crime and wars and lying and cheating and disease. There is bad stuff happening everywhere. How did we get into this mess? Well, you can be sure this wasn't what God planned, and it isn't what he wants for this planet. It happened because of bad choices. When Satan showed up looking like a serpent, he tempted Adam and Eve in the Garden and told them to disobey God, and they listened. They decided they knew better than God how things should be. They made the wrong choice. Big oops!

Everything started going wrong after that. People became selfish and mean. Nature turned against them. Weeds came up everywhere, and Adam and Eve and the rest of us had to do backbreaking work to clear the land. Storms, earthquakes and disasters happened. Rust, rot, terrible bacteria and parasites infested everything. All because Adam and Eve made the wrong choice, turned against God and sinned. What a mess! Is there any hope for us?

A Word from Josh and Sean

All of God's laws are for our own good. He designed humans, and he knows what makes us tick and how we can achieve the greatest happiness. If we follow his rules, we will come much closer to being what God wanted us to be. Joy, satisfaction and fulfillment come with obeying him. But God can't look at sin and not pay attention. He is perfect, and sin makes him angry. He can't be any other way—it is just the way he is. Because God is holy, he just can't respond any other way. He will always do what is right. God knew we would sin. He knew people would fail; so way back at the beginning of everything, he made a plan to bring us back to himself. That plan would save us from our sins. We'll learn more about his plan as we go through this book.

"When Adam sinned, sin entered the world. Adam's sin brought death, so death

spread to everyone, for everyone sinned" (Romans 5:1, NLT).

Q: Is Planet Earth doomed, or is it possible for our situation to change?

A: The answer to the "doomed" question is yes and no. Every day we hear about man-made damage and pollution and what it is doing to our planet. And it is true that we have not been as careful of our water and land and air as we should have been. When God created the world, he said everything was "good," and when God says something is good, it is the best it can be. Then sin came to the earth, and now, somewhere, something is just not right about the way things work on this earth. Much of what's wrong on the earth has been caused by greed and selfishness. Once Adam and Eve sinned, they couldn't stop sinning. And neither can we. Our sin, greed, selfishness and everything that goes with it has brought pollution not only to the earth but to our souls as well. But there is hope—lots of it. After Jesus was raised from the dead, he promised he would come back and set things right. And he will.

A Word from Josh and Sean

Many young people today have lives that show they live in a world that has stopped hoping for anything beyond tomorrow. The lack of purpose and direction that many young people demonstrate happens when God is rejected in favor of doing "what's right for me."

God let us go our own way when we wanted to sin. We are doomed to stay in that hopeless condition unless God himself makes the way for us to come back to him. How can we who are addicted to sin get back in his good graces? How do we find our way back to him? We can't do it unless he provides a way. But, thank God, he has done just that. He has reached down to us and given us a way out of our doom. As we answer more questions, you'll see what his plan is for us.

"God put the world square with himself through the Messiah, giving the world a fresh

start by offering forgiveness of sins" (2 Corinthians 5:18, THE MESSAGE).

Q: What's wrong with the idea that we should have as much fun as possible in this life?

A: Many young people think only about how to have fun—all the time. They hang out at malls. They go to one movie after another. They play endless video games. They are constantly texting on their phones. They sleep in as late as possible so they can do it all over again the next day. There isn't anything wrong with any of these activities. The problem is that many kids never think about doing anything else, especially when it comes to helping others. They don't have a mission in life. They don't have a reason for living, so they slide through their classes just to pass rather than putting in the effort to become excellent in their school subjects.

What often happens to these kids is that their lives feel empty. Some of them become sad and hopeless because life seems to have no meaning. While they want to be grown up and independent, when something disappoints them, there is nothing outside of themselves to focus on. People need other people, and kids whose only purpose in life is to pursue pleasure come up empty and lonely when times get tough.

A Word from Josh and Sean

Most kids growing up today have never known a world that puts duty to humanity before taking care of self. So they live a life that feels empty and lonely. It seems to have no purpose. Putting self first often results in depression for these kids. However, there is a solution to this lack of hope. The solution is to adopt a biblical worldview and find a purpose for your life. A biblical worldview simply means seeing life truthfully from God's perspective. Having a purpose will help you when times get tough and you are disappointed. Young people and adults alike need to understand clearly that God is calling them to see life from his perspective. It's the most direct path to happiness and joy, and even fun.

"Then he said to them, 'Watch out! Be on your guard against all kinds of greed; a man's life does not consist in the abundance of his possessions'" (Luke 12:15).

Q: Is God mean? Does he just want to spoil our fun?

A: God is *not* mean, and he would never spoil our fun—if our fun is not sinful. At the same time, he is holy, and he will not put up with sin. We can't just sin and get by with it. Lots of people try, but there will be a day when every person who has ever lived will stand before God and answer for his or her sins. When Adam and Eve disobeyed God's instructions and sinned, it's a wonder that God didn't fire off a couple of lightning bolts right there in the Garden of Eden and reduce them to twin piles of ash. And ever since Adam and Eve's disobedience, we have all sinned as well.

God is good and holy, and he cannot allow sin to exist in his universe. God didn't want to sentence us to eternity to be lost and without hope. Our sin had to be condemned, but he didn't want to condemn us. So he provided a way for us to get rid of our sin-- a way to bring us back to himself so that he could be friends with us. That's when Jesus, God's answer to our sin, came to earth. This wasn't any accident. God had planned before the world was even formed to send a savior to earth to save us from our sins. God always wants the best for us. He knows that when we are forgiven for our sins, we will find real happiness and fun—fun that is good fun and that brings us closer to him and to others rather than destroying us because it is wrong.

A Word from Josh and Sean

God is our heavenly father, and he is as delighted with his children as your parents are with you. Just as a mother delights in the smile of her infant, God delights in the love of his human creatures. He loved Adam and Eve with an incredible love and got great pleasure from being with them. This wonderful, joyful relationship between God and humans was meant to have love flowing continually in both directions. He created us for his delight, and he created us to delight in him. When man sinned, God could not stand the thought of losing us. He looked into the future, and just the thought that we would not be with him in heaven broke his heart. He wanted us to come back to him, so he made a plan to get rid of our sin and bring us back to him. That plan was Jesus. When Jesus died, he brought man and God back together to be friends.

"For there is one God and one mediator between God and men, the man Christ Jesus" (1 Timothy 2:5).

Q:Why can't God just ignore our sin?

A: Lots of people think that God is a kind old man who sits in heaven just waiting to hand out gifts to people whether they deserve them or not. Well, that's not a very accurate picture of our God. God is righteous. That means everything he does is right. He is just. That means every decision he makes is perfect and accurate. He is truth. That means he cannot lie. God doesn't sin, and he doesn't approve of sin in his children either.

God made a way for us to have our sins forgiven. He gave us the best and most precious thing he had—his Son, Jesus Christ. The only way to have our sins forgiven and removed from our lives is by making Jesus Christ our Lord and Savior. There is no other plan to make us right with God. So if we ignore his gift of salvation, and we decide to keep our sin, then God will punish us. He can't ignore our sin. He wouldn't be God if he looked the other way when it comes to our sin.

A Word from Josh and Sean

If God really loves us, as he says he does, why must he let sin stand between him and us? He's God, after all, and he's all-powerful, isn't he? He can do anything he wants, can't he? Why can't he just forget that we sin and save us anyway? The answer is because God is just. We have all fallen short of God's perfect measure. He cannot look on violations of his perfect rules and overlook sinners' actions. God must have perfection in his universe. Imagine what would happen if you went to court and the judge forgave a murderer and let him go free just because the judge wants to be loving. That's not right, and God always does what's right. God is truth, and his laws are righteous. God has to act by his own character to do what is right. He can't treat one sinner one way and another sinner a different way. He is fair and just to everyone.

"But may the righteous be glad and rejoice before God; may they be happy and joyful" (Psalm 68:3).

Q: God so loved the world, but does he love me?

A: The short answer is, "Yes, God loves you." He loves you just the way you are. He loves you even if you are sinful. He loves you no matter what you've done or said in the past. The Bible says that "God is love." That's what he's all about. His love isn't the easy kind of love that gives you everything you want. It's a tough love by which he gives you those things that are best for you. When Adam and Eve sinned, the first thing God did was to promise them a plan that would bring people close to him.

No one on earth truly understands the love of God. It is too big, too wonderful, too amazing for us to understand. We do know, however, that God's love causes him to come looking for us. It causes his Holy Spirit to make us uncomfortable in our souls until we are willing to respond to God's love. John 3:16 says, "For God so loved the world that he gave his one and only Son, that whoever believes in him shall not perish but have eternal life." God so loved the world—that includes everyone who has ever lived or who will ever live. God loved them all. That's the big picture. The small picture is that "whoever" (you, your friends, your family) believes in Jesus will have life that never ends. So God loves everyone, but he also loves each person individually. That's great news that should make all of us joyful.

A Word from Josh and Sean

To understand how much God loves us, you have to get involved. You really can't understand basketball until you play the game. You really can't appreciate a beautiful sunset if you never go look at one. There is a lot more enjoyment from a dance if you are the one dancing. In the same way, you have to participate in God's love to understand it. We will understand God's love when we trust him, and not before that. We can't just be spectators of God's story in the world; we have to get involved. If we really want to know his love, we have to be willing to apply his truth and love to our lives today. The Bible says that real love is this: "Not that we loved God, but that He loved us and sent His Son as an atoning sacrifice for our sins" (1 John 4:10).

"This is how God showed his love among us: He sent his one and only Son into the world that we might live through him" (1 John 4:9).

Q: What makes God angry?

A: Sin makes God angry. Now, he doesn't storm around heaven in a rage and cause lightning bolts to come down and strike people dead. But God is angry when he sees sinful actions such as children being abused and people stealing from each other and people fighting and killing each other. He knows that what he sees is a result of sin. He has provided Jesus to take away our sin. But so many people have no interest in being forgiven. They enjoy sinning, even though sin often makes them miserable. But God loves us, and instead of sending lightning bolts to destroy sinners, he sends the Holy Spirit to cause us to come closer to him. He's patient, and he waits for us to come to our senses and realize that his plan and his way are the best way to live on earth, and his plans will take us to heaven to live with him forever. Why not take a moment to thank God for his love and his patience. Spend a few quiet moments to see if he is calling you to a relationship with him.

A Word from Josh and Sean

Sin arouses God's wrath. It is not that he irrationally loses his temper because his plans for a perfect world are fouled up. There is nothing impulsive, random or changeable about God. He is not mean or angry. He is not trying to get even. His anger is not mysterious. His anger is controlled. His anger is only provoked by wickedness. He hates wickedness for what it does to the people he created and loves.

God is holy. That doesn't mean he's overly religious or a little strange. God just cannot stand sin. It is everything he is not. And he is everything sin will never be. Because God is pure, he cannot look at evil. We can be very glad that he provided a way for us to wash away our sins through the death and resurrection of his Son, Jesus. He died in our place and took the death penalty punishment we deserved. And he rose from the dead to show that we, too, can have eternal life through our relationship with him.

"God is a righteous judge, a God who expresses his wrath every day" (Psalm 7:11).

Q: Just what is real love?

A: Real love isn't the silly stuff we see in the movies and on TV. It isn't what your friends think it is when they talk about boyfriends or girlfriends. Real love is the kind of love God has for us. When humans rejected him and threw his love back in his face, he came back with more love. God chose the best thing in heaven as a gift to us—his Son, Jesus. He sent Jesus here to earth to be like us and love us and die for our sins. Love doesn't just mean giving gifts, it means giving yourself. You know how it is at Christmas or a birthday when someone gives you something just because he thinks he should. It doesn't mean a whole lot. But when that person takes the time to pick out a gift that will please you, or takes the time to make something special for you, it means a lot. That's because he is putting his time, energy and probably money—something of himself—into the gift he gives.

Do you think it would have meant as much to us if God had sent someone else—an angel or some other heavenly being—to be our savior? The most wonderful thing about what God did for us is that he gave us himself.

A Word from Josh and Sean

With all the personal disasters, worldwide poverty, floods, forest fires, earthquakes, terrorism, torture, disease, death and pain, many of us wonder why God would allow such terrible tragedies if he is really loving. We don't find any easy answers to this tough question. But God's Word shows us his love over and over again. When we understand God's love, we know we can trust him. And when we are ready to trust him, he will help us get above the pain and difficulties that may come into our lives. If you don't learn anything else from this book, learn that God loves you—eternally, completely. He loves you more than anything else he has created. He loves you with *real* love. You can count on it.

"This is real love: not that we loved God, but that he loved us and sent his Son as an atoning sacrifice to take away our sins" (1 John 4:10).

Q: What has God done for me?

A: He sacrificed everything he had and everything he was for your sake. Let me explain. God is powerful. Read stories in the Old Testament and you'll see his power dividing the Red Sea, sending plagues on Egypt and many other amazing events. But 2,000 years ago, when he wanted to show us his love, he laid down all his power and was born in a stable as the Lord Jesus. Then, when Jesus was grown and was hanging on the cross, some tormentors yelled for him to use his power and come down from the cross. Jesus refused to rescue himself. Jesus on the cross was God showing us his love rather than his power. Because he loved us so much, because he limited his power to save us, we get to live in heaven forever.

A Word from Josh and Sean

What God did for us by sending Jesus was to show how much he loves us. Real love shows itself as unlimited, selfless and risk-taking, with no guarantee of success. It opens itself up to being hurt if the love is rejected. God did it willingly. He opened himself up to the possibility of being rejected and hurt by you. God is strong, and perhaps the greatest show of his strength came when he limited his power and let himself suffer for us. He wasn't like the Romans who often enforced worship of their gods. In fact, Christians who resisted were often put to death by the Roman government. Jesus never forced anyone to believe in him. Instead, he tried to draw people to himself so that he could love them.

God was saying, "I love you so much that there is nothing I would not do to have a relationship with you. You are of infinite worth to me. I made you in my image and I want to know you in the same way I want you to know me. You are worth more to me than the lilies of the field, the snow-capped mountains and the fish of the sea. My love for you is limitless. I believe in you. I want to be part of your life. I want you to know the immense value I place on you. You can never consider yourself unloved or worthless. You are the dearly beloved of the God and creator of the universe."

"[Jesus] made himself nothing, taking the very nature of a servant, being made in human likeness. And being found in appearance as a man, he humbled himself and became obedient to death—even death on a cross!" (Philippians 2:6-8).

Q: If Jesus was God, why did he have to die?

A: Jesus *is* God, and he had to die for our sins because God the Father requires a blood offering to make up for sin. It has always been this way. But not just any blood sacrifice would take care of the sins of the whole world. Jesus was the only one who could satisfy God the Father's requirement for a perfect sin offering, once for all. In the Old Testament, priests offered a perfect lamb as a sin offering. That offering wiped away the people's sin for a year, but the next year and the next the offering had to be repeated. Then Jesus came to earth. He was called the Lamb of God, and when he died on the cross, he became the sin offering for all people, for all time. It was a sin offering that would never have to be repeated. Christ's sacrifice was for everyone who would believe in him as savior. Jesus was the perfect sacrifice who fulfilled all God's requirements for a sin offering. Today the only thing all of us must do is believe that what Jesus did on the cross when he died was enough. We have to accept his sacrifice for our sins. We have to confess that we are sinners and ask his forgiveness. Then he becomes the sin offering that takes away our sins, and God does not see our sin anymore. It is gone forever.

A Word from Josh and Sean

When Josh studied all the historical evidence about Jesus, he was convinced in his mind that Jesus *had* to be the one true God. But it was not knowledge that gripped his heart. It was the love of Jesus that caused him to commit his life to Christ. It was God's love that drew him to Jesus. Because Jesus died and was resurrected, we can know that our loving relationship with God will continue after death. Our new close relationship with God, made possible through Jesus' death on the cross, will continue beyond this life. God's incredible love caused him to find the solution for sin that would restore us to a relationship with him; and that solution was the life, death and resurrection of his only Son, Jesus.

"I have loved you, my people, with an everlasting love. With unfailing love I have drawn you to myself" (Jeremiah 31:3, NLT).

Q: What does the Bible teach about "resurrection"?

A: First, let's look at what the word "resurrection" means. The dictionary definition of resurrection is "rising from the dead." A second meaning is "a rising again from decay and disuse." The people in the Bible who were raised from the dead (like Lazarus) eventually had to die again. Jesus, however, rose from the dead to his perfect and eternal body. And that is what will happen to us one day—we will be given perfect and eternal bodies that will never decay, and we will permanently live in the presence of God.

In the meantime, Jesus said that if a seed falls into the ground, it has to decay for new life to come out of it. If you plant a seed of corn and then dig it up in a few days, you'll see that it is already starting to break apart with decay; but out of that seed you will see a sprout that will be the new stalk of corn. Our old bodies will get sick and we will die; but out of our death (for those of us who trust in Jesus) will come new life, and this will be a kind of life that never dies. It's really important that we believe that the resurrection of Jesus happened and that it will happen to us. Belief in the resurrection of Jesus is what makes Christianity different from all the other religions of the world. Christians cannot point to a tomb and say, "That's where Jesus is buried." The tomb of Jesus is empty. Hooray for God!

A Word from Josh and Sean

The resurrection makes it clear that no matter how awful our struggles, disappointments and troubles are, they are only temporary. In heaven, they won't matter anymore. Whatever happens to you, even if it is a tragedy or causes pain; no matter how sick someone in your family might be, and you are worried they might die; the resurrection promises you a future of good that can't be measured. Again and again the apostle Paul encouraged believers to focus on the life that never ends and not worry much about the troubles they have here in this life. The Bible makes it very clear in the Scripture below.

"The created world itself can hardly wait for what's coming next ... God reins it in until both creation and all the creatures are ready and can be released at the same moment into the glorious times ahead" (Romans 8:19-21, THE MESSAGE).

Q: Why is Jesus' resurrection important to me?

A: The resurrection of Jesus is important to all of us because it shows us that Jesus is alive today. He beat up on death, and he won. For Christians, Easter is the most important day of the year because on Easter we remember that Jesus not only came as a baby, but he is alive in heaven and knows what's going on in our lives here on earth. This is important because we have a hope for the future that people who don't know Jesus can never understand. Our faith is not some dead, dusty old religion with a dead guy in a tomb. Jesus promised all Christians that the best is yet to come.

A Word from Josh and Sean

Let's look again at the six reasons why you don't need to be afraid to die.

(1) *Death is mysterious and unknown,* but some of the mystery has been take away because Jesus died and left his footprints for us to follow right into heaven.

(2) *We have to face death alone.* That's true, but when we pass through the doorway of death, we'll find Jesus waiting there for us.

(3) *We are separated from our loved ones,* but it will only be for a short time. One day before long, Jesus will come back to

earth and take everyone who loves him to heaven with him. We will be with our loved ones forever.

(4) *We won't get to see our hopes and dreams come to pass.* Maybe not in this life, but our hopes and dreams come out of the abilities God has given us. Perhaps he will use our abilities, hopes and dreams in heaven.

(5) *Death might mean that we won't exist anymore.* The apostle Paul believed that everyone who belongs to Jesus will be given new life (see 1 Corinthians 15:20-22).

(6) *We can't avoid death.* Yes, death will come, but by now we hope you are convinced that we will go through death and come out safely in the arms of Jesus on the other side. And there is no better place to be.

"Neither death nor life ... nor anything else in all creation, will be able to separate us from the love of God that is in Christ Jesus our Lord" (Romans 8:38-39).

Q: Is heaven a real place?

A: Heaven is a real place where you will be with God and Jesus, and live forever. Sin won't be anywhere in heaven. Death is not the end; it is just the beginning. That is something we can really be happy about; but many people are not happy when they think of heaven. They think all we will do in heaven is sit around on clouds and strum harps. That's boring, and God isn't going to bore us. There is going to be work for us to do, and this work will be fun, because all of the things on this earth that hold us back will be gone. We won't have to learn how to do something. We will know how to do it. We won't be stopped in a project because we have no money. God owns all the wealth in the universe. There will be riches and wealth to help us with our projects. We will have all the time we need to do our work, and everything we do will be successful. Heaven will be a wonderful place to live, work and enjoy relationships with those we love.

A Word from Josh and Sean

Heaven is described as home. If you've ever been gone from home for a long time, isn't it wonderful when you finally climb into your own bed? That's the comfortable feeling heaven will give us. We will know we belong there. We will know that we are home. Heaven is a community. We will live together and be a family. Heaven will have the positive parts of an earthly city, but it will not have crime, poverty, pollution, slums and corruption. It will be a beautiful place. Heaven is a place of rest. Even when we work hard there, we will not get tired, because we will be doing something we love for work.

"However, as it is written: 'No eye has seen, no ear has heard, no mind has conceived what God has prepared for those who love him'" (1 Corinthians 2:9).

Q: What is heaven like?

A: First of all, heaven is the place where God lives and where we will live with him—forever! That should give you goose bumps. Second, there will be no sin in heaven. We won't be tempted to do anything wrong, because Satan will not be there to put tempting thoughts into our minds. It's a place where everything you desire to do can be accomplished. There will be no restrictions on your talent.

Money will not be a problem—there won't even be money, but there will be all the riches God provides. We don't know what those will be yet, but they will be good, because everything God does is good. There will be work for us to do—work that fits our talents and abilities. And once you get to heaven, you will never want to come back to earth. You will be completely satisfied.

Jesus said he was going away to prepare a home for us. He said that in his Father's house are many rooms. He also said that when it is ready, he will come back and take us to be with him. Heaven sounds like a wonderful place to be.

A Word from Josh and Sean

Our work in heaven will be restful because it will fit us perfectly. It will be exactly what

we love to do and can do best. Have you ever had a time when you felt that what you did was exactly right and it was the best work you had ever done? That's a wonderful feeling, and it is only a small taste of what work will be like in heaven. As a result of our work in heaven, we will experience the most peaceful and fulfilling rest imaginable. No more frustration. No more struggling to get it right.

Here is a big thing to remember: We may not be able to picture everything about our new life in heaven, but this we can be absolutely sure of: God created us for his delight. He created the earth for our delight and pleasure. All our earthly pleasures are spoiled now, because Adam and Eve sinned in the Garden. But in heaven, everything that was created will be restored. Because God loves us so much, he wants us to experience all the delights he originally intended when he created us for his love.

"I am going there to prepare a place for you. And if I go and prepare a place for you, I will come back and take you to be with me that you also may be where I am" (John 14:3).

Q: Sometimes I doubt there is a heaven. What can I do about that?

A: Well, one thing you can't do is go to heaven and check it out. You can't send a friend to check it out either, but you can read a kind of travel book that tells you what heaven is like and how to get there. The Bible acts as a road map to help us find the gateway to heaven, where we will have a home forever.

Of course, if you don't read and study the Bible, you won't have a clue what's in it and you won't know how to get to heaven. You won't have a road map. Maybe someone will fill you in on the route to heaven, but if that doesn't happen, you might miss the crossroad that puts you on the right road.

The Bible has all the answers to your questions. Read it every day; and when it is hard to understand, pray and ask God to help you understand. He wants you to know what's in his Word more than you want to know. He *will* help you.

A Word from Josh and Sean

When John the Baptist was in prison, he had some serious doubts, first about Jesus and then about heaven. Jesus sent word to remind John of what Jesus knew was in John's heart—the truth. Jesus told John's disciples to go back to John and tell him what they had seen and heard. The blind have received their sight, the lame walk, the lepers are cleansed, the deaf hear, the dead are raised up and the poor have the gospel preached to them. Jesus provided truth that he was the one the world had been waiting for—he was the Messiah. John could trust Jesus—all the way to heaven. If we have doubt of anything regarding Jesus and heaven, we just have to keep remembering what we already know is true. Jesus came to make a way for us to go to heaven where we will be with him.

"Now this is eternal life: that they may know you, the only true God, and Jesus Christ, whom you have sent" (John 17:3).

Q: Will I be a ghost floating in space?

A: There's a lot we don't know about heaven, but we do know that you will *not* be a ghost. We know that because Jesus, when he came back to life, was not a ghost. Some of his disciples doubted that he was alive again. Some of them thought he was a ghost, but he said to them, "Why are you troubled, and why do doubts rise in your minds? Look at my hands and my feet. It is I myself! Touch me and see; a ghost does not have flesh and bones, as you see I have" (Luke 24:38-39).

That should be enough to convince us that Jesus came back to earth with flesh and bones that look much like ours. It was a different kind of body because his body could pass right through walls. Several times he either appeared to his disciples who were gathered behind closed doors, or he disappeared when he was inside with them. He was there and then he was just gone. We can't help but wonder what passing through walls will be like when we are resurrected. But if we are going to be like Jesus, we will be able to do what he did after he was resurrected.

A Word from Josh and Sean

We will have physical bodies when we are resurrected. God has prepared for us new bodies, and those flesh-and-bone bodies will need a solid, physical environment filled with oxygen and edible food on which to survive. Paul doesn't tell us that we will be bodiless spirits. Indeed, he says the opposite. We will have bodies—real bodies like those we have right now—but they will be immortal. We will not catch diseases; we will not grow old; and we can never die again. Our new bodies will be like the newly created bodies of Adam and Eve, absolutely perfect in every detail, very beautiful, immensely strong, utterly healthy; and they absolutely cannot age or die.

"[The Lord] will swallow up death forever" (Isaiah 25:8).

Q: I've heard that someday there will be a new earth. Will it be a real place?

A: Yes, the new earth is a real place—a wonderful place you are going to love. Are you confused because the Bible says that when we die we will go to heaven, and now all of a sudden we are talking about a new earth? What's that all about?

In the book of Revelation in the Bible, the writer John says he saw a new earth coming down out of heaven to earth. He said: "And I heard a loud shout from the throne saying, 'Now the dwelling of God is with men, and he will live with them. They will be his people, and God himself will be with them and be their God. He will wipe every tear from their eyes. There will be no more death or mourning or crying or pain, for the old order of things has passed away'" (Revelation 21:3-4).

So the new earth will be a place where God and his people live together forever; and when we get there, God's going to take away all our sadness. How does that sound to you?

A Word from Josh and Sean

We will be resurrected with physical bodies to live on a new earth, where God will come down to live with us. We will be surrounded by beauty, with real gardens, cities, kingdoms, rivers and banquets. We will call this new existence "heaven" because that is what it will be. But it will be light years away from the idea a lot of people have of heaven being a place so boring that no one would want to go there.

We may not be able to picture everything about our new existence in heaven, but we know this: God created us for delight and pleasure. "Delight" means something that gives us great pleasure. Some of that delight and pleasure got pretty messed us when Adam and Eve sinned; but God is going to give back to us what he first intended. He loves us deeply and he wants us to experience everything he intended when he created us.

"For my Father's will is that everyone who looks to the Son and believes in him shall have eternal life, and I will raise him up at the last day" (John 6:40).

Q: What will the new earth be like?

A: Sometimes on this earth, we get a tiny glimpse of what heaven might be like. When we see a beautiful scene in nature, or there's a day when everything has gone well and we are content and happy, it seems as if those might be glimpses of heaven. The new heaven and the earth will be breathtakingly beautiful. There will be no terrible storms to tear up homes and leave people stranded. There will be no earthquakes or fires to ruin everything. There will be no weeds or thorns or insects to eat our plants. Animals will not harm us. Imagine scratching behind the ears of a tiger or petting a porcupine. That will be a new and exciting experience. There will be no pollution, so colors will be brighter than anything we have ever seen. There will be no erosion and no plant diseases, and our pets will not die. The new earth will be so wonderful that we will never want to be anywhere else again.

A Word from Josh and Sean

The Bible talks about the New Jerusalem as part of the new heaven and the new earth. This city is one of dazzling beauty. Cities are full of inhabitants, streets, buildings, cultural events, entertainment, athletics and other community gatherings. If the New Jerusalem were not a real city, why would the Bible refer to it as a city? Heaven will be like the most beautiful city on earth, without the crime, poverty, pollution, slums and corruption that mar cities in this world. Let your mind go to think up the most beautiful city and place you can imagine. Heaven is going to be far, far better than anything you can think of. It's surely something you don't want to miss.

"I saw Heaven and earth new-created. Gone the first Heaven, gone the first earth, gone the sea. I saw Holy Jerusalem, new-created, descending resplendent out of Heaven, as ready for God as a bride for her husband" (Revelation 21:1-2, THE MESSAGE).

Q: How can I be sure I will get to heaven and also live on the new earth?

A: Way back there when Adam and Eve goofed up and brought sin into the world, God had a plan to restore his people to himself. That's the whole reason why Jesus came to earth, died an awful death and was resurrected. His actions opened the door to heaven for us. All we have to do is believe in what he has done for us and ask his forgiveness for our sins. Then we can be assured that heaven will be our home. If you have never asked for God's forgiveness, all you have to do is confess that you have sinned and ask God into your heart. That's all there is to it. Praying this prayer, and meaning it, can and will change your life forever. You've just made the most important decision of your life.

A Word from Josh and Sean

Christ's resurrection has defeated sin and Satan—the cause of all problems. God is in control. There is a beginning to the story of God's love for us and there is an ending that we haven't seen yet. We are in the middle of the story, and sometimes when we are in the middle of something, it is hard to make sense of what will happen at the end of the story. God wants as many people as possible to pray the prayer you have just prayed. He wants them to be restored to him too. He wants to bring them into his family. He is raising an army of Christians to participate with him in overcoming sin and making the world right again.

"Count yourselves dead to sin but alive to God in Christ Jesus" (Romans 6:11).

Q: Is there any sin that is too terrible for God to forgive?

A: There is no sin too terrible for God to forgive. Think about the apostle Paul. He held the coats of people as they killed Stephen, a good man who had done no wrong. Think about Peter. He lied not just once but three times when he said he didn't know Jesus, because he was afraid he would be crucified along with Jesus. Peter and Paul are not unusual cases. All through the Bible we find stories of people just like Peter and Paul, and just like us, who failed God and sinned. But those people found their way back to God and asked his forgiveness. God forgave them and brought them into his family.

When we sin, God understands that we are weak. He knows that we are going to make mistakes. But as long as we want to follow him, as long as we hate our sins and turn to God for forgiveness, he forgives us. The key to it all is to know that we have sinned, to be sorry for what we have done and to confess our sin to God, accept his forgiveness and turn away from our sin. When we do that, God throws open his arms to welcome us home to him.

A Word from Josh and Sean

Even though we sin, we never give up the opportunity to live a full Christian life. When we turn our hearts back to God, he will reach out and embrace us in his loving arms, restoring us in our relationship with him. That's what Jesus did after Peter denied him three times. And this is what Jesus will do for us as well. We are his children, and he loves us greatly. Paul says, "So you are no longer a slave, but [God's own child]. And since you are [his child], God has made you also an heir" (Galatians 4:7). An heir is someone who inherits everything his father has. That is the new life God offers—the new life we can have in him in spite of our sin and rebellion against him.

"For the wages of sin is death, but the gift of God is eternal life in Christ Jesus our Lord" (Romans 6:23).

Q: How do we know that Jesus really came back to life?

A: In other words you are asking, *Is it true? Can I believe it?* Well, no one who is alive today saw Jesus after he came back from the dead. However, even though no one alive today has seen him in his resurrected body, there is a lot of evidence to say it is true. First, there is the witness of more than 500 people who saw him after his resurrection. Many of them wrote about their experience. Ancient law said there only needed to be three or four witnesses to an event. Also, there is an empty tomb rather than a tomb with a dead man inside. In Mecca, there is a tomb where Muslims say their prophet Muhammad is buried. Buddha has a tomb too. In fact, all the other "gods" people have worshiped over the years have tombs with their gods in them. Only Christianity has an empty tomb. But perhaps the most important evidence of Jesus' resurrection is the change in a person's life when he or she believes in Jesus Christ as savior. Life for that person is never the same again.

The Bible tells us that Jesus rose from the dead. We either have to believe that fact is true or throw out the whole Bible. We can't pick and choose what we want to believe and reject the rest. We have to believe it all, and that means believing that our savior lives today.

A Word from Josh and Sean

It is important for you to decide what you will believe about Jesus' resurrection. Deciding that his resurrection is true can change your life here on earth and forever. The writers of the New Testament encouraged us to make up our minds about whether Jesus came back to life or not. They urged us to accept the truth they knew to be real—that the resurrection was a real event. Once you believe, it is then important to respond to Jesus by looking to him for answers and guidance in this life. Will you fall on your knees, as the disciple Thomas did when he saw Jesus alive again, and say, "My Lord and my God"? The answer to this question is very important.

"I know whom I have believed, and am convinced that he is able to guard what I have entrusted to him for that day" (2 Timothy 1:12).

Q: What does it mean in my everyday life that Jesus was resurrected?

A: Because Jesus is alive, we have someone to really love us. No other religion will tell you of a God who loves us so much that he left heaven to come to this messed-up earth and die for us so that he could be with us forever.

We have someone who accepts us just the way that we are. God died to make us ready to live with him forever.

We have someone who understands us better than we understand ourselves. Jesus came to earth to be like us and experience everything we do. Just like you, he got hungry and cold and tired and felt alone. No one understands us as well as he does.

We have someone who is with God and is representing us to God the Father. When the devil comes with an accusation against us, Jesus is right there to defend us.

We have someone we can look forward to seeing in heaven, where we will be with him forever. There, we will be like he was after he was resurrected. We, too, will have flesh-and-bone bodies as he did when he appeared to the disciples.

A Word from Josh and Sean

Christianity gives us a real solution to our problem of dying. It makes it possible for us

to live forever. Christianity is the only religion that gives us the deep desires of our heart. Christianity is a complete religion that gives us answers for life here and for our forever life.

The resurrection of Jesus is the key to all the promises God has made to us. The promises of eternal life wouldn't have any meaning and would never happen if Jesus had not been raised from the dead. But Jesus beat death and showed us that we can do it too. If there had been no resurrection, then what we believe is worthless. Because Jesus came back to life, because it is true, we can be sure that everything Jesus has promised about heaven will happen for us.

"[Jesus is] there from now to eternity to save everyone who comes to God through him, always on the job to speak up for them" (Hebrews 7:25, THE MESSAGE).

Q:What is a miracle?

A: People often say about some remarkable event that it is "a miracle." Sometimes we say it when our parent finds a parking space in a crowded parking lot. Sometimes we say it's a miracle when we get an *A* on a test when we did not study. Well, those are wonderful events, but they are not miracles. Miracles are when God steps in and changes what naturally would have happened. Jesus did true miracles when he lived on earth. He spit on the ground, mixed it with dirt and rubbed the mud on a blind man's eyes, and the man could suddenly see. Blind people do not get their sight again unless there is a miracle. Jesus went to the house of Jairus and raised his daughter from death. That's a miracle, because dead people normally stay dead. Miracles help us realize that God has great power, and that great power is working on earth today.

A Word from Josh and Sean

One man said there are five things that a true miracle must have to be a miracle. Those five things are:

(1) *A miracle is a one-time event.* When Jesus was raised from the dead, it was a one-time event that truly showed God's power.

(2) *A miracle goes against the ordinary course of events.* The resurrection of Jesus was a supernatural event that doesn't happen on an everyday basis. Dead people normally stay dead.

(3) *A miracle interrupts order.* You will only recognize a miracle if you first believe there is order to all that happens on earth.

(4) *A miracle must be the result of the power of God.* So if you go to a doctor and have an operation that restores your sight, that is a wonderful event, but it is not a miracle.

(5) *A miracle is a sign that God is acting and overriding the way things normally work.*

"I will remember the deeds of the Lord; yes, I will remember your miracles of long ago" (Psalm 77:11).

Q: Are there really miracles that are happening today?

A: You betcha! The greatest miracle of all was the resurrection of Jesus from the dead. There are some people who don't believe in miracles because when a miracle happens, it doesn't follow some idea or rule of nature they have in their heads. Their minds are closed to truth. That isn't good thinking. In the last few years, scientists have discovered many things about nature that were never known before, and they are hard to believe even when proved.

When the duckbill platypus was discovered, scientists closed their minds to the truth that such an animal could exist. They thought it was a fake. The creature laid eggs, so they thought it was a reptile, but reptiles have skin and this creature had fur. In addition to laying eggs, it also had webbed feet and a bill like a duck; but it wasn't a duck. It wasn't until someone brought a platypus that was about to lay eggs to the scientists in London that they had to believe, because the proof was right in front of their eyes.

You see, because God made the rules of nature, he can break them if he wants to. He can do the miraculous, and he will do that when it suits his purpose.

A Word from Josh and Sean

One time when Josh was invited to speak to a class, he presented the evidence that Jesus was God and that Jesus had been resurrected from the dead. The professor started to ask angry, hostile questions and make accusations about the resurrection. A student asked, "Sir, what do you think happened that first Easter?" The professor replied, "I don't know, but it wasn't a resurrection!" That professor's mind was closed to truth. "Is your answer the result of looking at all the evidence?" the student asked. "No!" the professor replied. This is the attitude of many people regarding miracles, and especially the resurrection. They are unwilling to believe in the resurrection of Jesus because they have concluded in advance that miracles cannot happen. But is this good reasoning? Wise people follow the evidence wherever it leads.

"We will not all sleep, but we will all be changed—in a flash, in the twinkling of an eye, at the last trumpet. For the trumpet will sound, the dead will be raised imperishable, and we will be changed" (1 Corinthians 15:51-52).

Q: How many trials did Jesus have?

A: Jesus was questioned six separate times before his execution. Three of these took place in the Roman court, and three took place in the Jewish court. Here they are listed:

1. Before Annas, the Jewish high priest
2. Before Caiaphas, the priest who had been appointed by the Romans
3. Before the Jewish council—the Sanhedrin
4. Before Pontius Pilate, the Roman governor
5. Before Herod
6. Before Pilate again

A Word from Josh and Sean

Why was there all this fuss over one man? There was a fuss because both the Romans and the Jews were concerned about Jesus going around the country preaching. Many of the Jews thought that what Jesus was teaching was false. One thing Jesus said that upset the Jewish leaders was that he was stronger than the Temple, and since the Temple was one of the most important places to the Jews, they were worried about him taking over and replacing their Temple. Jesus also said he was the Messiah. The Jews believed the Messiah was going to drive the Romans out of Israel. Because they didn't believe Jesus was the Messiah, they were afraid he might start a revolutionary war, and if that happened, Rome would come down hard on them. Last of all, Jesus pleaded guilty to all the charges they had made and then said he was equal with God. What he said made the Jewish leaders furious with him. They wanted him punished. They wanted him to die.

"Jesus stood before the governor, and the governor asked him, 'Are you the king of the Jews?' 'Yes, it is as you say,' Jesus replied" (Matthew 27:11).

Q: In what way was Jesus' trial and guilty verdict a mockery?

A: Jesus was the perfect Son of God. He had no sin in him. The rulers of Israel, and Pontius Pilate of Rome, had no reason to put him to death. But Jesus threatened everything the Jewish leaders were and everything they believed. So the rulers called in witnesses to give false evidence. At first they couldn't find anyone to say lies against him. Then they found people who came forward and said, "This fellow said, 'I am able to destroy the temple of God and rebuild it in three days.'" Jesus had made that statement, but he had not been talking about the stone temple that stood in Jerusalem. He had been speaking about his own body that would die and in three days be raised from the dead.

The witnesses and rulers didn't get it. They thought Jesus was saying that he was more important than God. When they asked him if he was the Son of God, and he answered that he was, they thought he was saying bad things against God and their religion. The rulers missed who Jesus truly was. Rather than truly investigating the character of Jesus and the truth of his words and his meaning, Pontius Pilate more or less went along with what they were saying. The whole trial was a mockery, a joke.

A Word from Josh and Sean

Jesus was accused of sedition (any action in speech or writing that promotes discontent or rebellion) by the Jewish religious rulers. He was brought for trial before the Roman governor, Pontius Pilate. History shows that Pilate was extremely cruel and merciless. He was stubborn, proud, corrupt, brutal and spiteful. One historian says that Pilate was responsible for all kinds of terrible evil deeds against the Jewish people.

He often had people killed without any trial at all. Pilate wanted to get rid of Jesus for different reasons than the rulers did. Pilate saw Jesus as a threat to his rule. When Jesus said he was king of the Jews, Pilate couldn't take any chances. If Jesus truly were the king of the Jews, it would brand him as an enemy of Caesar. Jesus had to die.

"You are my Son; today I have become your Father ... I will be his Father and he will be my Son" (Hebrews 1:5).

Q: What grounds for conviction finally condemned Jesus to death?

A: Of the six charges of which Jesus was accused, he was finally convicted of claiming to be the Son of God. The Jewish leaders thought he was lying. They considered his words to be blasphemy. The word "blasphemy" is not one we use much today. In fact, you might never have heard the word before. It means: an act of cursing God or assuming you have the rights and qualities of God. It is ungodly behavior toward anything that is holy. It is a very serious charge, and Jewish law demanded death to the one who blasphemed. Because the Romans ruled Israel at the time of Jesus, the Jews had to go to them to get a death sentence. They were not allowed to put someone to death. Pilate believed Jesus was a troublemaker stirring up the people; and because Jesus said he was a king, he was a threat to Caesar. So Pilate convicted him and sentenced him to death.

A Word from Josh and Sean

While the Jews were concerned about the religious part of what Jesus had said while teaching the people, the Romans were more concerned with politics, economics and the authority of Rome. When Jesus answered Pilate's question, "Are you the king of the Jews?"

by saying, "It is as you say," he gave them grounds for execution. To say that Jesus was a king was to imply that Caesar was not. When Jesus said, "My kingdom is not of this world," Pilate probably did not understand what he meant. But he could take no chances. If Jesus truly were the king of the Jews, that would make him an enemy of Caesar. Jesus had to die to prevent him from stirring up trouble and threatening the rule of Caesar in Israel.

"The angel said to Mary: 'You will ... give birth to a son, and you are to give him the name Jesus. He will be great and will be called the Son of the Most High. The Lord God will give him the throne of his father David, and he will reign over the house of Jacob

forever; his kingdom will never end'" (Luke 1:31-33).

Q: How was Jesus killed?

A: This is not a happy story, but it is an important story—the most important story ever told. Jesus was killed by crucifixion. Crucifixion was a terrible, brutal execution used by the Romans. They did not invent it. It had been used as a method of execution for at least 700 years before Jesus died on a cross. Most often it was used for slaves or rebels or to discourage uprisings. The pain of this kind of death was so terrible that a new word was invented to describe it. That word is "excruciating." It means "out of the cross." The cross was bad enough, but before his death on the cross, Jesus was beaten so severely that his wounds probably would have killed him if he had not been crucified. To further insult him, the soldiers jammed a crown of thorns on his head. Then, in that condition, he was forced to carry the crossbeam of his own cross to the hill where he was crucified. Jesus was a mass of bleeding, suffering flesh. What's so amazing about this story is that he went through all of this willingly. He became the perfect, sinless sacrifice for our sins. He is a wonderful Savior!

A Word from Josh and Sean

The Jews knew that Jesus had predicted his own resurrection. They were afraid that his followers might do something to make it appear that Jesus had died and risen again. So the Romans took extraordinary precautions to be sure he was dead and remained dead. By crucifying Jesus on a hill outside Jerusalem, his death became very public. Anyone walking by on the road would have seen him hanging there on the cross. No one could say he had not died. Even after Jesus appeared to be dead, one of the Roman executioners thrust a spear into his side. Blood and water flowed out. The separation of blood and water in the bloodstream is a sure sign of death. Four executioners had to report to Pilate that Jesus was indeed dead. The fact that Jesus was truly dead is an important part of the story of his resurrection. Because he was truly dead, he was truly resurrected. We can rejoice that he is a living Savior.

"Dogs have surrounded me; a band of evil men has encircled me, they have pierced my hands and my feet" (Psalm 22:16).

Q: What happened to Jesus' body after his death?

A: After Jesus died and the soldiers had proved that he was dead, his friends got permission to take the body down from the cross and bury it. Joseph, a rich man who came from an area of the country known as Arimathea, asked Pilate for the body. Joseph was a disciple of Jesus but had not made that fact public because he was afraid of the Jewish leaders. Nicodemus, another of the Jewish leaders, went with Joseph to claim Jesus' body.

It was the custom to wrap a body in linen with a mixture of myrrh and aloes, two sweet-smelling spices. Very near where Jesus was crucified, Joseph had a new tomb in which no one had ever been buried. Because it was the day before the Sabbath when the Jews were not supposed to do any work, the two men had to hurry to get Jesus' body ready and into the tomb. Some of the women disciples watched them put Jesus into the tomb. They planned to come back after the Sabbath day to finish a proper burial. After the body was ready, the two men rolled a stone in front of the door of the tomb, and everyone went home to observe the Sabbath.

A Word from Josh and Sean

We can be very sure that Jesus was buried in Joseph's tomb. Paul says the story is true and he would have seen documents that told about the death of Jesus. The story of the burial is told in a simple way. The story has not been expanded to be more exciting. No documents have ever been found that speak against the burial story as told in the Gospels. The Jews who had wanted to get rid of Jesus for a long time paid attention to where he was buried. One professor who has studied the death and burial of Jesus says that Jesus' burial in the tomb is one of the earliest and most true facts about Jesus. Jesus died on the cross and he was buried in a tomb. Of that we can be sure.

"He was assigned a grave with the wicked, and with the rich in his death, though he had done no violence, nor was any deceit in his mouth" (Isaiah 53:9).

Q: Where was Jesus buried?

A: Jesus was buried in a tomb carved from solid rock. Inside the tomb there was a stone bench that went around three sides of the tomb. Jesus' body was laid on the bench. Tombs like this were usually for people of high rank. Since Joseph of Arimathea was a member of the ruling class of Jews, his tomb was of this type. The tomb door was covered by a disk-shaped stone. The stone was huge and was held in an open position until it was time to close the tomb. It rested in the higher part of a channel dug along the front of the tomb. When it was time to roll the stone into place, the wedge holding it in place was removed and the stone rolled down to cover the door. Jesus was made ready for burial inside this kind of tomb.

A Word from Josh and Sean

Many people have tried to find ways to say that Jesus never died and was never buried. You see, if he did not die as Scripture says, then they don't have to believe that he was ever resurrected. So we need to look carefully at history and see if what is recorded truly happened to Jesus. We need to see if what is recorded about his burial goes along with the burial customs of the time.

The Jewish leaders and the Roman officials wanted to make sure that Jesus' body stayed in the tomb. The officials took several security precautions to prevent people from taking Jesus' body and then saying he had come back from the dead. But all their precautions did not prevent Jesus from being resurrected. And for that we can be glad.

"But God raised [Jesus] from the dead, freeing him from the agony of death, because it was impossible for death to keep its hold on him" (Acts 2:24).

Q: How did his friends prepare his body for burial?

A: The Jews had a particular way of burying their dead. Here's what happened. Jesus was taken down from the cross and wrapped in a sheet. He had to be buried before sunset because there was no work allowed on the Sabbath, and he died the day before the Sabbath, which began at sundown on the previous day. Two men, Nicodemus and Joseph of Arimathea, got his body ready for burial. It was a quick preparation because it was almost the Sabbath. They washed his body with warm water. We don't know if it happened to Jesus, but in many cases the fingernails of the dead person were cut and cleaned and the hair arranged. Then the body was wrapped in strips with spices, starting at the feet and continuing up to the neck. A separate cloth was placed over the head. At least part of this preparation was done, but we know it was not completed, because women were coming back on the first day of the week to complete the burial preparations; that's when they discovered the empty tomb.

A Word from Josh and Sean

The New Testament is very clear that the burial of Christ followed the customs of the Jews. Jesus was taken down from the cross and covered with a sheet. The Jews were quite strict about not allowing the body to remain all night upon the cross. So Jesus was taken to the tomb of Joseph of Arimathea. It was the custom, as verified in the New Testament, to prepare the corpse (after cleansing) with various types of aromatic spices. In the case of Christ, 75 to 100 pounds of spices were used. That wasn't a great amount for a leader. When King Herod died, 500 servants carried the spices used in his burial.

First, the body was straightened then clothed in grave clothes of white linen. The cloth used could not have ornaments or stains. Each person was buried in three separate garments. At this point, sweet smelling spices, which were a sawdust-like compound known as aloes, were mixed with a sticky substance called myrrh. The body was wrapped in the linen cloths with spices placed between the folds of the fabric. It's important to us that just as Jesus was actually dead and was actually raised from the dead, one day we, too, will die and be raised from the dead.

"Taking Jesus' body, the two of them wrapped it, with the spices, in strips of linen. This was in accordance with Jewish burial customs" (John 19:40).

Q: Why was a two-ton rock put in front of the door of Jesus' tomb?

A: The Gospel writer Mark said that the stone put over the door to the tomb was "extremely large." While it was easy to roll the stone downhill in the trench made for that purpose, it would take a lot of men to roll it back uphill so that the tomb would be open. That little detail—that the stone must be rolled uphill to open the tomb—is important when we read what Matthew wrote. He said there was an earthquake and an angel rolled back the stone. When an earthquake happens and there is no angel involved, things roll downhill. They don't roll uphill. What happened with the stone was truly a miracle. Jesus' body was put inside a tomb behind a stone where it would be difficult for anyone to get it out. Anyone, that is, but God's angel. On that Sunday morning when the women came to the tomb, they found it open. The heavy stone had been rolled back uphill and an angel was sitting on it. The tomb itself was empty. Jesus was gone.

A Word from Josh and Sean

After a lecture Josh gave at Georgia Tech University, two engineering professors went on a tour of Israel with other faculty members. They remembered the comments Josh had made about the enormous size of the stone. So, being engineers, they took the type of stone used in the time of Christ and calculated the size needed in order to cover the doorway of the tomb. Later, they wrote Josh a letter telling him about all their careful calculations. They said a stone of that size would have had a minimum weight of one-and-one-half to two tons. That's 1,500 to 2,000 pounds. The large stone would have provided additional security against the Jewish suspicion that the disciples of Jesus would try to steal his body.

"There was a violent earthquake, for an angel of the Lord came down from heaven and, going to the tomb, rolled back the stone and sat on it" (Matthew 28:2).

Q: Why was a Roman guard of 16 men assigned to watch the tomb?

A: There had been rumors that the disciples planned to steal the body of Jesus and claim that he had been raised from the dead. To keep that from happening, Pilate posted a guard at the tomb. The Roman soldiers who were guarding the tomb were not like the security guards you see guarding buildings at night. These were tough, highly trained soldiers. Each guard was trained to protect six feet of ground. Sixteen men in a square of four on each side were supposed to protect 36 yards of earth. It worked this way: four men were placed immediately in front of what they were to protect. In this case it was the tomb of Jesus. The other 12 would sleep in a semicircle in front of them with their heads pointing toward the middle of the semicircle. If someone wanted to steal what the guards were protecting, they would have to walk over the guards who were sleeping and then confront the four who were awake. It wasn't going to happen. There was no way that the disciples or anyone else would have been able to steal the body of Jesus from the tomb.

A Word from Josh and Sean

The Jewish authorities told Pilate that they wanted a guard posted because they had heard of Jesus' prediction of his own resurrection.

They feared that his disciples would steal the body to make it appear that Jesus had been raised from the dead. The Jewish authorities—the high priest and the ruling body—would have known what Jesus had said since they were always searching for evidence to convict him. They probably did fear the consequences of a successful plot to simulate a resurrection. So they went to Pilate and said, "Sir, we remember that while he was still alive that deceiver said, 'After three days I will rise again.' So give the order for the tomb to be made secure until the third day. Otherwise, his disciples may come and steal the body and tell the people that he has been raised from the dead. This last deception will be worse than the first." Pilate granted their request. He said to the guard, "Go, make the tomb as secure as you know how" (Matthew 27:62-65). Sealed tombs mean nothing to God when he is ready to move forward with his plan and work.

"For as Jonah was three days and three nights in the belly of a huge fish, so the Son of Man will be three days and three nights in the heart of the earth" (Matthew 12:40).

Q: Why did Pilate put a seal on Jesus' tomb?

A: When Pilate told the soldiers to make the tomb as secure as they knew how, they set a seal on the tomb. A seal was made of string and clay. The string—cord—was stretched across the rock and fastened at either end with sealing clay. The clay was impressed (stamped) with the official seal of the Roman governor Pilate. If anyone tried to move the stone, the seal on one or both ends would be broken and the authorities would know someone had tampered with the stone. The body of Jesus was protected not only by 16 Roman soldiers but also by the official seal of the local ruler of Rome. No one could open that tomb, steal away the body of Jesus and then say that he had risen from the dead. So what happened there?

A Word from Josh and Sean

In ancient times, seals were used to authenticate something. "Authenticate" means "to prove something is real." When the tomb of Jesus was sealed, it proved that his body was being guarded by the authority of the Roman Empire. Anyone who broke the seal by moving the stone would have brought down the anger of Roman law on himself. It was serious business. An ancient marble slab was discovered with a warning to grave robbers. It read, "By ordinance [law] of Caesar. It is my pleasure that graves and tombs remain perpetually undisturbed ... let it be absolutely forbidden for anyone to disturb them. In case of violation, I desire that the offender be sentenced to capital punishment [death] on charge of violation of sepulcher [tomb]." No one who valued his life would have moved that stone. Something else happened to the stone and the seal.

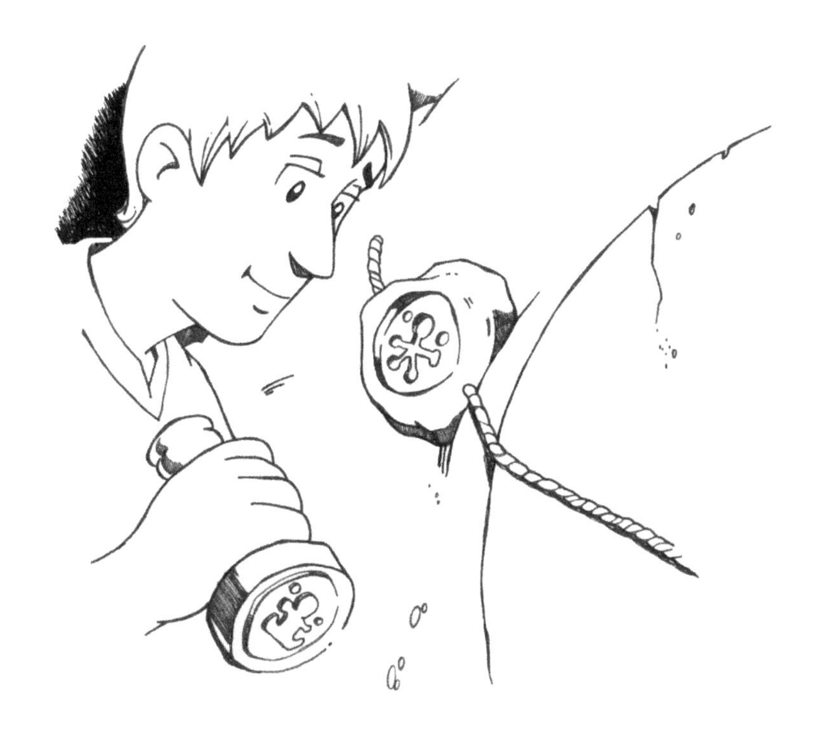

"The angel said to the women, 'Do not be afraid, for I know that you are looking for Jesus, who was crucified. He is not here; he has risen, just as he said'" (Matthew 28:5-6).

Q: What happened to the guards at Jesus' tomb?

A: Remember those guards at the tomb who would die if they didn't do their duty and protect the tomb? Perhaps you are wondering what happened to them. Remember how tough they were supposed to be? Well, they took off. They fell asleep, woke up to find an empty tomb and deserted their post. They left the tomb. The punishment for leaving a post of duty was death. These guys failed miserably. What happened to keep them from being killed was that the guards went to the Jewish officials and told them what had happened. The chief priests came up with a plan. They gave the soldiers a large amount of money to say that the disciples had stolen the body of Jesus while he was asleep. They said that if the governor heard about it, they would keep the soldiers out of trouble.

A Word from Josh and Sean

A soldier who left his post would be punished by death. Therefore, soldiers were very careful to pay attention to duty—especially night duty such as they had at the tomb of Jesus. If robbers had come to rob the tomb, the stone would have simply been rolled on down to one side. The position of the stone would have proved that the guards were sleeping when they should have been guarding the tomb. But the fact that the stone had been rolled uphill proved to the Jewish authorities that what had happened at the tomb was humanly impossible. Something more powerful than grave robbers had moved the stone. They knew what the guards said was true. The Jewish priests knew that they couldn't let word get out that something supernatural had happened there, so they bribed the guards with money to hush them up.

"For we know that since Christ was raised from the dead, he cannot die again; death no longer has mastery over him" (Romans 6:9).

Q: Who was the first person to see Jesus alive?

A: Jesus appeared first to his friends. The women disciples were the first ones to know about his resurrection, and it was probably Mary Magdalene who was the first person to see him alive. Do you remember that when Jesus was buried just before the Sabbath, those who buried him were in a hurry? On Sunday morning, the women returned to the tomb to complete the burial preparations. Because these women lived in a small nearby town, they probably didn't know that the stone had been rolled across the door after Jesus had been put inside. They didn't know they wouldn't be able to get in. They also didn't know that a guard had been posted to keep anyone from opening the tomb and going inside. It didn't matter what had happened after they left, because when they arrived, the tomb was open and an angel was there, telling them to go tell the disciples.

A Word from Josh and Sean

Mary went early to the tomb, and when she found it open, she began to cry. She went and told Peter and John. They came, looked in and saw that what she said was true. They left, but Mary stayed. She was crying. As she wept, someone came up to her and asked why she was crying and who she was looking for. She didn't realize it at that moment, but the person speaking to her was Jesus. What a joy to see that someone you knew had been dead was now alive and walking around!

The first appearance to Mary Magdalene happened early in the morning. She was outside in the garden where the tomb was located. Mary was alone when she saw him. She was overwhelmed with emotion and crying. It wasn't until Jesus spoke her name that she recognized him.

"He is not here; he has risen, just as he said. Come and see the place where he lay" (Matthew 28:6).

Q: When people went to Jesus' tomb, what did they find?

A: What they didn't find was Jesus' body. It was gone. What they did find were the grave clothes in which he had been wrapped. Remember, when answering an earlier question about how Jesus was prepared for burial, we learned that there were three parts to the grave clothes. We also learned that the body had been wrapped up to the neck in linen strips. Gummy spices were wrapped in as well, and that made the strips stick together. Unwrapping a body would have been a long and difficult task, taking quite a bit of time—more time than a tomb robber would have had. A tomb robber would have taken the whole thing—body and grave clothes. The head had been covered with a separate cloth. What the disciples found was the grave clothes still wrapped up and the headpiece folded and laid to one side. Jesus was gone, and he had left his grave clothes right where they were. Now the disciples knew that Jesus was alive. That was the only thing that could have happened to find the grave clothes there but his body gone.

A Word from Josh and Sean

Even though there was no body in Christ's tomb on that Sunday morning, the tomb was not totally empty. It contained an amazing phenomenon. After visiting the tomb and seeing the stone rolled away, the women ran back to tell the disciples what they had seen. Then Peter and John took off running. John ran faster than Peter, and upon arriving at the tomb, he did not enter. Instead, he leaned over and looked in and saw something so startling that he immediately believed that Christ had indeed risen from the dead.

He looked over to the place where the body of Jesus had been. There were grave clothes, in the form of the body, slightly caved in and empty—like the empty chrysalis of a caterpillar's cocoon. Seeing that would make a believer out of anybody! John never got over what he saw.

"For as in Adam all die, so in Christ all will be made alive" (1 Corinthians 15:22).

Q: Who else saw Jesus alive after his death and burial?

A: Over the next few days, all the disciples saw Jesus alive. They were in different places and in different circumstances when they saw him.

There were two disciples walking to a town called Emmaus about seven miles from Jerusalem. They were talking about everything that had happened during the last few days. As they walked and talked, Jesus came up to them and walked along with them. They didn't recognize him. After all, who would be looking for someone they knew was dead to come and walk with them? He asked them what they were talking about. They couldn't believe that this stranger didn't know what had happened in Jerusalem. They told him that they believed that Jesus was a prophet who had come to set Israel free, but now he was dead. It happened three days ago. They told him that the women had gone to the tomb and found only grave clothes.

When they got to their town, Jesus acted as if he would go on, but they asked him to dinner. When he was at the table with them and he took bread, gave thanks, broke it and began to give it to them, they recognized him. As soon as they did, he disappeared.

A Word from Josh and Sean

A lawyer named Tom Anderson said, "Let's assume that Christ did not rise from the dead. Let's assume that the written accounts of His appearances to hundreds of people are false. I want to ask you a question. With an event that was so well publicized, don't you think that if Jesus had not risen from the dead, at least one eyewitness would record that he had seen Christ's body in the tomb? He might have said, 'Listen, I saw that tomb—it was not empty! Look, I was there; Christ did not rise from the dead. As a matter of fact, I saw Christ's body.' But there is no such witness against the resurrection." Jesus is alive! Those two disciples on the road knew it. As soon as they realized that Jesus was alive, they went straight back to Jerusalem, found the disciples and said, "It is true! The Lord has risen and has appeared to Simon." Then they told the disciples the whole story.

"Were not our hearts burning within us while he talked with us on the road and opened the Scriptures to us?" (Luke 24:32).

Q: How many people saw Jesus after his resurrection?

A: Only two or three witnesses were required by Jewish law to convict someone of a crime. The chief priest found only two false witnesses to testify against Jesus. It was enough to convict him. The apostle Paul says in the Bible that after Jesus was resurrected, more than 500 people saw him alive, including all of his disciples. Most of those witnesses were still alive at the time Paul was writing the account (see 1 Corinthians 15:6). Five hundred witnesses is more than enough proof according to Jewish law that Jesus is alive. In fact, it seems that Paul is saying, "If you don't believe the resurrection happened, go ask those witnesses who saw him."

Do you ever wish you could have been among those who saw Jesus alive after his resurrection? What would you have asked him if you had seen him? What would you have talked with him about? Someday, in heaven, you will be able to ask him anything you want and you will be able to spend as much time as you want talking with him.

A Word from Josh and Sean

When you write a report about an event in history, it is important that there are a group of people still living who saw the event happen.

A large number of witnesses helps prove the accuracy of the published report. For instance, if we all witness a murder, and in a week the police report turns out to be a bunch of lies, as eyewitnesses we can speak out against the report. So when a book is written about an event, eyewitnesses or participants can say for sure that the event happened. When the book of 1 Corinthians was written, there were enough people still alive who had seen Jesus resurrected to prove that he really did rise from the dead. If each of these 500 people were to testify in a courtroom for only 6 minutes, you would have 50 hours of firsthand eyewitness testimony. Then add the testimony of many other eyewitnesses and you would have a very convincing argument that Jesus was resurrected.

"God has raised this Jesus to life, and we are all witnesses of the fact" (Acts 2:32).

Q: Some people say it was a myth that Jesus came back to life. Why is it not a myth?

A: Many people try to find another explanation for Jesus' resurrection than the true one that he came back to life. They make up all kinds of ideas to explain what happened at the tomb in Jerusalem. Some of the things they make up are harder to believe than simply believing what the Bible says: Jesus came back to life on the third day after his death.

One theory (idea) about Jesus' resurrection is that it was a myth—a myth like the ones about the Greek gods. A myth is a story, usually with a hero who does something that cannot be explained by natural rules. It is an invented story or an imaginary thing or person. So those who believe that the story of Jesus is a myth don't believe he died and rose again to save them from their sins. That's sad. Be thinking about what you believe about the resurrection.

A Word from Josh and Sean

The people who say Jesus' resurrection was a myth don't realize how much true evidence there is about his resurrection. Their arguments are weak. The death and resurrection of Jesus Christ took place within history, at a specific historic time. It was the time of Roman rule in Israel. He was tried before Pilate. Pilate has been proven to be a historic figure. Myths, on the other hand, are not historical. They are often tied to annual events in nature like the longest or shortest day of the year. They are not tied to events that actually took place. It doesn't make sense that the apostle Paul would be out there preaching a pagan religion. He frequently spoke out against pagan religions. Paul would not have spent his life preaching a made-up religion. Instead Paul preached that Jesus rose from the dead. He was even willing to die for that message.

"We weren't, you know, just wishing on a star when we laid the facts out before you regarding the powerful return of our Master, Jesus Christ. We were there for the preview! We saw it with our own eyes" (2 Peter 1:16, THE MESSAGE).

Q: There is something known as an "Unknown Tomb" theory. What is that?

A: One of the earliest theories presented to explain away the resurrection is that the actual tomb of Jesus was unknown. Some believe this today. The believers of this theory say that Jesus was a criminal, and criminals' bodies were not buried but were thrown into a pit. So they believe Jesus' body was thrown into a common pit for the executed rather than put in a new tomb as the Bible says. But historians say that the Jews were allowed to bury their dead even if the person had been crucified. A historic discovery proves this. In 1968, the remains of a Jewish man were found in a family tomb outside Jerusalem. He had been crucified and he had been buried in a tomb.

A Word from Josh and Sean

This theory ignores the history of Jesus' death and resurrection as recorded in the Bible. Jesus' body was prepared according to Jewish customs and then was laid in a tomb. If no one else knew where the tomb was, Joseph of Arimathea and Nicodemus knew. They were the ones who prepared the body and put it in the tomb. Not only did Joseph and Nicodemus know the location, so did the disciples and priests, the Roman soldiers and many people of the time when Jesus was buried.

The unknown-tomb idea does not fit or explain all the facts. What happens is that people want to believe in the unknown-tomb theory, so they go looking for facts to prove their idea. A better way is to look at all the facts and then decide what happened. If an event in history is approached this better way, truth will be learned about that event. If honest people do this, they will come to the conclusions that Jesus was buried in a tomb as the Bible says.

"I will praise you, O Lord my God, with all my heart; I will glorify your name forever. For great is your love toward me; you have

delivered me from the depths of the grave" (Psalm 86:12-13).

Q: Others believe a "Wrong Tomb" theory. Why is that theory not true?

A: The wrong-tomb theory is a little like the unknown-tomb theory. It says that when the women returned to the tomb on Easter Sunday morning, they went to the wrong tomb. These people believed that the women did not know where Jesus was buried. If that were true, the enemies of Christianity would have rushed straight to the "right" tomb and opened it to prove Christ was still in the tomb. The women knew the correct tomb. Of course, Jesus did rise from the dead, just as the angel said to the women: "He is not here! He is risen" (Luke 24:6).

A Word from Josh and Sean

The women had carefully noted where the body of Jesus was buried. This wasn't a public cemetery, but a small private burial ground. How could anyone who cared as much as these women cared forget where a dearly beloved one was buried? To believe this theory, one would have to say that not only did the women go to the wrong tomb, but so did Peter and John and other Jews and Romans who were checking to see if the tomb really was empty. You would even have to say that the angel appeared at the wrong tomb. That doesn't make any sense at all. Jesus has risen, just as he said he would.

"He [Jesus] was assigned a grave with the wicked, and with the rich in his death" (Isaiah 53:9).

Q: Why is the "Legend" theory not true?

A: First of all, let's learn what a "legend" is. A legend is a story that cannot be proved to be the truth. Often these stories are about someone who is greatly admired. An example of a legend is that George Washington chopped down the cherry tree and then told the truth when his father asked him if he did it. No one knows whether that story is true or not, and it probably is not. Legends are usually handed down from one generation to the next. They start out as stories told sometimes to make a point. The George Washington story is told to say that George was a truthful boy. But as these stories are told again and again, people begin to believe they are the truth. A legend has begun. Jesus' resurrection is not a legend, but some people say it is. There are too many people who saw Jesus alive again after dying to say the resurrection is merely a legend.

A Word from Josh and Sean

It is impossible for the resurrection to be a legend. Accounts of the event were written down by original eyewitnesses and circulated throughout the known world. Remember all those eyewitnesses to Jesus' resurrection?

Legends take a long time to develop. Several generations of people have to come and go before a legend is believed. Paul wrote only three to eight years after Jesus' death and resurrection about the eyewitnesses who had seen him alive again. Three to eight years is not enough time for a legend to grow and be believed. At that time, there would have been many people still living who remembered what actually happened. If the story had been changed, they would have spoken up to set the record straight.

There are many legends about other religious leaders such as Buddha and Muhammad, but it took hundreds of years for these legends to be formed and for people to believe them. It is not a legend that Jesus rose from the dead.

"It has always been my [Paul's] ambition to preach the gospel where Christ was not known ... as it is written: 'Those who were not told about him will see, and those who have not heard will understand'" (Romans 15:20-21).

Q: Some say that only Jesus' spirit rose, and not his body. Why is that not true?

A: This is called the "Spiritual Resurrection Theory" and it is wrong. This idea is that Christ's body decayed in the grave and the real resurrection was only his spirit. He was more like a ghost than like the person the disciples knew and loved. Today there is a very well-known religion that believes this theory. This religion believes that God destroyed Jesus' body in the tomb and that he rose in a body that didn't have flesh and bones. But if Jesus didn't come back in a body, then why did the disciples and those 500 others who saw him believe that he had a real body that they could see and touch? Either we believe everything the Bible says about Jesus and the resurrection, or it's all a lie. When we believe that Jesus is alive, it changes our life and gives us hope for a better life that will last forever.

A Word from Josh and Sean

When Jesus appeared to his disciples, he scared them. They thought he was a ghost. Jesus said, "Look at my hands and my feet. It is I myself! Touch me and see; a ghost does not have flesh and bones, as you see I have" (Luke 24:39). Later on, Jesus ate fish with his disciples, further showing us that he had flesh and bones. Spirits don't eat fish. And another time, Jesus appeared to some women as they ran to tell his disciples he was alive. "Greetings," he said to them. They grabbed his feet and worshiped him (see Matthew 28:9). You don't grab the legs of a spirit! Jesus was real, and he had a body.

The apostle Paul believed in a physical resurrection and he said that some day we too will be raised with a physical body. Those new bodies will be different than the ones we have now, but they will be real—physical.

"For the wages of sin is death, but the gift of God is eternal life in Christ Jesus our Lord" (Roman 6:23).

Q: What is the "Hallucination" theory?

A: One of the theories that just won't go away is that the witnesses only *thought* they had seen a risen Jesus. This theory believes that they were hallucinating. "Hallucinate" means that someone sees something in his or her mind that is so real to them that they believe it really is happening when it is not. So when the disciples were accused of hallucinating, they were told that the resurrection really didn't happen. The accusers said that what the disciples thought they saw only happened in their minds. If you believe this theory, then everything the Bible says about the resurrection really didn't happen.

Usually people who have hallucinations are either mentally ill or have taken some drug that causes the hallucination. But in the Bible story, the people were ordinary people who were not mentally ill. There were fishermen and shopkeepers and teachers who saw Jesus alive again. They were not crazy and they had not taken drugs. They were not hallucinating.

A Word from Josh and Sean

It would be stretching the truth to believe that all those people, the 500 witnesses, had the same hallucination. Two people could not have the same hallucination any more than two

people could have the same dream. You can't ask someone to join your dream.

After his resurrection, Jesus sat down with people and ate with them and invited them to touch his body. A hallucination doesn't do that. Also, hallucinations usually come to people who are expecting something wonderful to happen, and that's what causes them to hallucinate. However, the disciples did not anticipate Jesus being resurrected. They were not expecting anything so wonderful to happen. They thought he was dead and gone forever.

There is nothing real about a hallucination. If the disciples had a hallucination about Jesus' death and resurrection, there would have been no empty tomb, no broken seal, no guards and no high priests to try to cover up what really happened. It is so much easier to believe that what the Bible says is true—Jesus died, was buried and rose from the dead to live forever—than to believe the hallucination theory.

"The next day John saw Jesus coming toward him and said, 'Look, the Lamb of God, who takes away the sin of the world!'" (John 1:29).

Q: What is the "Jesus Swooned and Was Revived" theory?

A: The swoon theory is that Jesus really did not die on the cross. When someone swoons, he or she faints or loses consciousness. So those who believe the swoon theory believe that Jesus merely fainted. They believe that when he was nailed on the cross, he went into shock and lost consciousness. The theory goes on to explain that people in that time didn't have the medical knowledge to tell the difference between death and a swoon. They believed Jesus was buried alive and the cold tomb revived him. And his disciples (who believed he had died) couldn't believe the cold air of the tomb brought him back to consciousness. Instead the disciples insisted that Jesus had been resurrected from the dead. But the swoon theory just can't be true. Let's let Josh and Sean tell us why.

A Word from Josh and Sean

The problem with this theory is that it doesn't recognize what Jesus had been through. Here are some of the facts that help us believe that Jesus really died on the cross and did not swoon:

(1) The terrible wounds he suffered from beatings, lack of sleep, a crown of thorns jammed on his head and his collapse on

the way to the cross were severe enough to kill him.

(2) What happens at crucifixion makes sure the person is dead on the cross.

(3) When his side was pierced, blood and water poured out, and that is medical proof that Jesus was dead, because blood and water separate at death.

(4) Jesus knew he was dying when he called out to Father God, "Into your hands I commit my spirit" (Luke 23:46).

(5) The Roman soldiers were trained killers, and when they went to break Jesus' legs so that he would die more quickly, they found out he was already dead. They did not need to break his legs.

(6) Pilate sent a centurion to make sure Jesus was dead before he gave the body to Joseph of Arimathea.

(7) Jesus' body was wrapped in about 100 pounds of linen strips and spices. He could not have breathed, much less gotten up and come out of the tomb.

(8) If he were not already dead before being placed in the tomb, he would have died of lack of water, food and medical treatment.

(9) Even non-Christian historians say Jesus died on the cross.

The truth is that Jesus died on the cross, and he was resurrected as our living Lord.

"For God so loved the world that he gave his one and only Son, that whoever believes in him shall not perish but have eternal life" (John 3:16).

Q: There is even a "Muslim Substitution" theory. What is that?

A: The Muslim holy book, the Koran, says that Jesus was not crucified on the cross. It says that Allah respected his prophet Jesus (Muslims believe that Jesus was a prophet, and not God's son) and saved him by substituting a bystander who was made to look like Jesus who was then crucified. That's why it's called the "Substitution Theory."

The Koran goes on to say that instead of being crucified, Jesus ascended to heaven, where he remains alive until his return to earth before the end of time. However, that can't be true because Jesus himself said that he would die for the sins of all people. Nowhere in the Bible does it say that someone would be substituted for the Christ in death. Of course, if you believe this theory that Jesus did not die, then he could not be resurrected.

If God's plan had always been to take Jesus to heaven without death, then why would some other person have been substituted and made to die? When Mary and the disciples stood looking up at the dying man, they believed it was Jesus on the cross and not a look-alike. God wouldn't have put them through Jesus' death if his plan had always been to have a substitute die on the cross. The whole thing simply doesn't make sense.

A Word from Josh and Sean

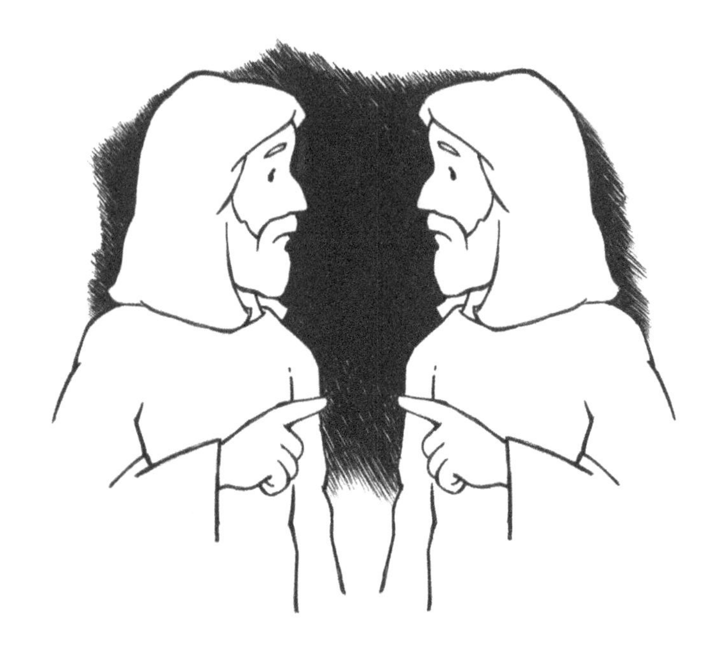

Think about this. Muslims believe that Jesus is not God, but a prophet. If Jesus said he would die a violent death and then did not, but escaped by substitution, then Jesus lied and is a false prophet. The argument looks like this:

1. Jesus predicted his violent death.
2. If Jesus died a violent death, then the Koran is wrong since it says he escaped death by substitution.
3. If Jesus did not die a violent death, the Koran is wrong again when it says that Jesus is a prophet. If he did not die the way he said he would, he is a false prophet.

Those who propose this theory (and the other theories) try to prove that Jesus did not die on the cross for our sins. But all the evidence says he died exactly as the Bible said he did and he was also resurrected just the way the Bible said.

"Your faith in God has become known everywhere ... they tell how you turned to God from idols to serve the living and true God, and to wait for his Son from heaven, whom he raised from the dead—Jesus" (1 Thessalonians 1:8-10).

Q: Did the disciples steal Jesus' body and then say he was raised from the dead?

A: This is one of the earliest theories trying to prove that Jesus had not risen from the dead. In fact, the rulers of the Jews gave the Roman soldiers a large sum of money to lie. The rulers told them, "You are to say, 'His disciples came during the night and stole him away while we were asleep.' If this report gets to the governor, we will satisfy him and keep you out of trouble. So the soldiers took the money and did as they were instructed. And this story has been widely circulated among the Jews to this very day" (Matthew 28:12-14).

The disciples were scared to death of both the Romans and the Jewish leaders. They would not have had the courage to attempt to steal the body, and the leaders knew that. They made up the story about the disciples stealing the body to protect the soldiers. Unfortunately, that story has stayed around from then until now.

A Word from Josh and Sean

Those who are dead set against believing in the resurrection have found many ways of dealing with the hard fact of the empty tomb. But remember that (1) any explanation must take into account all the facts, and those facts have to fit together; and (2) you can't decide what happened and then go look for facts to support what you believe. You have to first look at all the facts and then decide what happened.

If the disciples had stolen the body of Jesus, they would all have had to agree on what happened and would never have been able to tell the truth. It would have been a conspiracy. What usually happens when there is a conspiracy is that eventually someone slips up and tells the truth and the conspiracy falls apart. But every one of the disciples told the same story—that Jesus had been resurrected from death. And it has never been proven that anything else happened. They all stayed true to the story they told about the risen Christ until they died.

"God has raised this Jesus to life, and we are all witnesses of the fact" (Acts 2:32).

Q: Who in his right mind would die for a lie?

A: All of the disciples except for John died a martyr's death. That means they were put to death for what they believed about Jesus. The disciples never wavered in saying that Jesus truly did rise from the dead. They died for the truth—that Jesus is alive. They knew they had not stolen the body of Jesus. They knew they had not forgotten the location of the tomb. They knew that Jesus had not swooned and come back to life in the cool tomb. They were so sure about the resurrection of Jesus that they made preaching about it the most important part of their message. Because they believed Jesus was alive, they were willing to die for preaching about his resurrection.

A Word from Josh and Sean

One big problem with the idea that the disciples stole Jesus' body and hid it is that it doesn't fit the kind of men the disciples were. They were men of honor. Jesus taught them to tell the truth and to live good, honorable lives. Stealing a body and lying about it would not be honorable. The apostles were sincere men who soon began to teach the gospel; and because what they taught seemed true, those who listened became Christians, and the new church began to grow like crazy. What they taught about Jesus eventually cost the disciples their lives. They died for what they believed. If they had been lying, at any time they could have said so and delivered the body of Jesus to the authorities and saved themselves. But there was no body to give to the authorities. Jesus had risen.

"They were longing for a better country—a heavenly one. Therefore God is not ashamed to be called their God, for he has prepared a city for them" (Hebrews 11:16).

Q: What evidence points to Jesus' resurrection?

A: In this book we've talked a lot about the evidence that points to Jesus' resurrection. Much of that evidence is what we call "circumstantial evidence." Circumstantial evidence happens when a lot of facts are given but none of them are as clear as someone saying, "I saw what happened." In the case of Jesus' death and resurrection, there are lots of pieces of circumstantial evidence such as worship on Sunday, baptism, Communion, the radical change in the Jewish customs and the martyrdom of the disciples. When you put all that circumstantial evidence together, it proves that Jesus came back to life. In a court of law, when a trial is going on, circumstantial evidence is just as valuable as direct evidence. (Direct evidence is when someone says, "I saw it happen.") *Strong* circumstantial evidence can be trusted more than direct evidence because it cannot be made up as easily.

A Word from Josh and Sean

"Circumstantial evidence" means that a jury draws its conclusions of guilty or not guilty not from a single fact—such as someone can prove he saw another person kill someone with a gun—but from the circumstances surrounding the case. For example: *Direct evidence* is when a man testifies that he saw the man pull a gun and shoot a clerk. That evidence deals directly with the fact. But if the evidence shows that (1) the man was seen entering the store immediately before the shooting; (2) a sales slip shows he had purchased the gun; (3) his fingerprints are on the gun and the cash register; and (4) tests show that the bullet came from his gun, it is all *circumstantial evidence.* All these facts together prove to the jury that the robber is guilty of the crime.

"Believe me when I say that I am in the Father and the Father is in me; or at least believe on the evidence of the miracles themselves" (John 14:11).

Q: Why is the resurrection celebrated 52 times a year?

A: When you go to church on Sunday morning, you are celebrating the resurrection. Before Jesus rose from the dead, the Jews celebrated the Sabbath—the seventh day of the week. After Jesus came back to life on the first day of the week, Sunday, the disciples decided to change their day of worship from the Jewish Sabbath to Sunday. That is probably one of the most important decisions ever made by a group of people in history. The Jews believed that if they didn't keep the Sabbath and all its rules, God would punish them. So for them to throw that teaching away and start worshiping God on a different day of the week was a big step. It said the old religion was gone and everything was new.

A Word from Josh and Sean

The early Christians were Jews who kept the Sabbath carefully. The Jews, including the new Christians, were afraid of breaking the Sabbath rules. They believed that if they broke the strict laws about how to keep the Sabbath, God would be furious with them and something awful would happen to them. Yet the new Christians were so sure that Jesus had risen from the dead on the first day of the week that they changed their day of worship to Sunday.

The resurrection of Jesus Christ became a weekly celebration. Can you think of any other historical event that is celebrated 52 times a year? The reason for this weekly celebration is that Jesus appeared personally to these people after his resurrection, convincing them he was alive.

"On the first day of the week we came together to break bread. Paul spoke to the people and, because he intended to leave the next day, kept on talking until midnight" (Acts 20:7).

Q: Why is water baptism a celebration of the resurrection of Jesus?

A: Baptism is a picture of the actual burial and resurrection of Jesus, and it is one of the things Jesus left for his people to do to show the world they are believers. Everyone who believes in Jesus should be baptized to show others that their lives are going to be different now. If you have never been baptized in water, talk to your parents about doing this. Or set up a time to talk with your pastor about the importance of water baptism. There are many different ways that churches baptize believers. Some churches take the believer into a lake or pool or a tank of water called a baptismal tank. The believer is put all the way under the water when he or she is baptized. Some churches sprinkle the head of the believer to symbolize going under the water. Others pour water over the head. It isn't so much the way the baptism is done as what it means. It means that you have decided to be a Christian and follow Jesus for the rest of your life. It means that you never intend to turn back from following Jesus.

A Word from Josh and Sean

Baptism in the early church came out of the Jewish practice of people cleansing themselves in pools of water before entering the Temple to worship the Lord. Baptism is called a sacrament—a sacred duty or obligation. Baptism is meaningful because Jesus died and was raised from the dead. Water baptism is like a picture of what happened to Jesus when he was buried in the tomb and then raised up. When the believer goes down into the water, it is as if he is being buried. When the believer comes up out of the water, it is as if he is being resurrected to a new life. People have been baptized in water all the way back to the early church. Baptism is a way for a person to say he or she is a follower of Jesus.

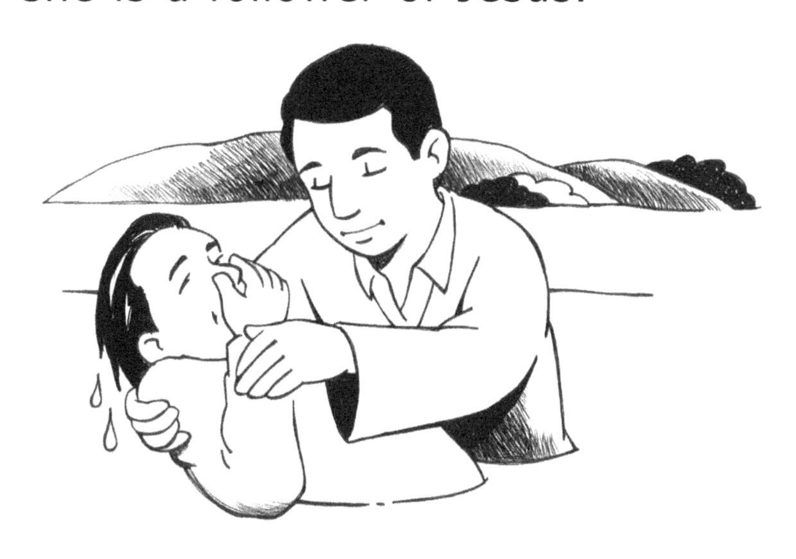

"We were therefore buried with him through baptism into death in order that, just as Christ was raised from the dead through the glory of the Father, we too may live a new life" (Romans 6:4).

Q: Why is Communion a celebration of Jesus' death and resurrection?

A: Just before Jesus died, he gathered his disciples together for one more meal with them. It was at that time that he gave them a ceremony to help them remember that he had died for their sins, their healing and that he would come again to take them to heaven. We call this ceremony "Communion" or "the Lord's Supper."

Jesus took ordinary food items. He took a piece of bread and broke it in pieces and gave the pieces to his disciples. He said, "This is my body given for you: do this in remembrance of me." Then he took a cup of wine and said, "This cup is the new covenant in my blood which is poured out for you." Churches today use bread or crackers, and wine or grape juice. It really doesn't matter what is used for Communion; what's important is remembering what Jesus did for us on the cross.

A Word from Josh and Sean

Communion is another sacrament in which the cup and bread symbolize Christ's death on the cross and the shedding of his blood for the sins of mankind. Believers got together regularly to remember that Jesus had been publicly slaughtered in a terrible and humiliating way. When believers take part in Communion, they show others the great joy they have that Christ died for them personally. How could great joy go along with knowing about the horrifying death of the founder of Christianity unless there was a resurrection to bring joy? Communion, remembering the death of the founder of Christianity, only makes sense if our leader, Jesus, is alive today. And you can be sure that Jesus is alive today!

"Whenever you eat this bread and drink this cup, you proclaim the Lord's death until he comes" (1 Corinthians 11:26).

Q: How did Jewish believers' lives and customs change once they knew Jesus had been resurrected?

A: The Jews are people who have always kept strict laws about their diet, their worship and, in some cases, even the way they dress. When other groups of people married outside of their religion, their faith and identity disappeared. They became like the people around them. But the Jews have always kept themselves separate from the people who live around them. Their customs are very important to them because they believe that God gave them their customs. They believe that if they abandon these customs, their souls might end up in hell. However, after Jesus was resurrected from the dead, the Jewish Christians abandoned their religious rituals and laws and switched to worshiping God in the Christian way. This huge change in their lives and customs is another of the "circumstantial evidences" that Jesus rose from the dead.

A Word from Josh and Sean

Only five weeks after Jesus was crucified and raised from the dead, more than 5,000 people believed he was the Messiah. They were willing to give up or change their ancient beliefs to follow him. Here are some of the changes they made:

(1) The new believers never again sacrificed an animal for their sins. They believed that Jesus was the perfect sacrifice for their sins.
(2) The new believers gave up some of the rituals of their old religion.
(3) The new believers began to worship the Trinity—three Gods in one: God the father, God the son, God the Holy Spirit.
(4) The Jewish people had been expecting their Messiah to be a military leader. They had not been expecting someone like Jesus who had come to suffer and die for them. Yet, after Christ's resurrection, the early Christians believed that Jesus was the Messiah who had come to suffer and die for them before being resurrected.

They no longer looked for a military deliverer.

The disciples were willing to give up their old traditions and were willing to die for their new beliefs.

"An angel of the Lord opened the doors of the jail and brought [the apostles] out. 'Go, stand in the temple courts,' he said, 'and tell the people the full message of this new life'" (Acts 5:19-20).

Q: What made the believers change from fearful cowards to people who were willing to die for what they believed?

A: One of the most amazing parts of the circumstantial evidence about Jesus' resurrection is that men who were cowards became willing to die for their faith. There was Peter who stayed in the courtyard while Jesus was tried and told a lie three times to a servant girl. He said he didn't know who Jesus was. But don't be too hard on Peter. The other disciples disappeared completely. They ran off. They were nowhere to be found. At least Peter stuck around. After Jesus' resurrection, and before they knew he was alive again, all the disciples were hiding from the Jews when suddenly Jesus appeared to them. Yes, they were cowards. Then in the next few days something amazing happened to them. Let's see what it was.

A Word from Josh and Sean

What changed the disciples from cowards to brave men was seeing Jesus resurrected. They didn't change to gain wealth or to be more important in their culture, that's for sure. They changed because the living Jesus was standing right in front of them. The rewards they got for believing that Jesus was alive again and for preaching it everywhere were beatings, stonings, being thrown to the lions and every other means the authorities could find to try to stop them from talking. None of it worked. Those disciples just went right on telling everyone they met about Jesus. Finally they died for what they believed and preached. Why were they willing to die for what they believed? Because when they saw Jesus alive again, their lives were changed forever.

"Be strong and courageous. Do not be afraid or terrified because of them, for the Lord your God goes with you; he will never leave you nor forsake you" (Deuteronomy 31:6).

Q: What do you believe in your heart about the resurrection of Jesus?

A: We are almost at the end of this book. We've learned a lot of facts about Jesus' resurrection. We've learned that without a doubt Jesus was crucified, buried and rose from the dead. We've learned that any information presented as fact must have eyewitnesses or strong circumstantial evidence, or both, and that the resurrection of Jesus has both. We've seen what happens to believers when the truth of the resurrection gets into their hearts—how it turns cowards into brave men who are not afraid to preach the gospel. Now it's time to think about what each one of us believes in our heart about how Jesus came back to life to save us from our sin and to give us an eternal home in heaven. If all we do is think about what we've learned, it doesn't do us any good. We have to take what we've learned and believe it in our heart—way down deep inside of us. When we believe with all our heart, it will change us, just the way it changed the disciples.

A Word from Josh and Sean

Sean says, "I believe with confidence that Jesus really walked the earth, did miracles, died on the cross and rose from the grave on the third day. I believe that the resurrection shows conclusively that Jesus is God (see Romans

1:4). I believe that it is because of the resurrection that we are empowered by the Spirit of God (see Philippians 3:10), and that we no longer have to fear death (see 1 Corinthians 15). Jesus is the creator of the universe, who loves us intimately. He died on the cross and rose from the grave so that we could be restored into a relationship with him." You can believe with confidence too.

"I am not ashamed, because I know whom I have believed, and am convinced that he is able to guard what I have entrusted to him for that day" (2 Timothy 1:12).

Q: If you have not taken action to make Jesus your Savior, what do you plan to do about it?

A: You can believe all kinds of things, but they never change your heart and life unless you take action on what you believe. Jesus said that even demons believe in him and tremble. We won't be meeting any demons in heaven even though they believe. Why? Because what they believe in their heads never gets down into their hearts. So how do we get this information about Jesus from our heads to our hearts and let it begin to change us?

Here's how in three easy steps. First, confess that you are a sinner. That shouldn't be too hard, as the Bible tells us that "all have sinned and come short of the glory of God" (see Romans 3:23). Second, believe that Jesus is God's Son given as a sacrifice to take away your sins. The Bible says that we have been "justified by his grace through the redemption that came by Christ Jesus" (see Romans 3:24).Third, ask Jesus to take away your sins and make you clean and pure in your heart (see 1 John 1:7).

A Word from Josh and Sean

If you live on this earth and don't make Jesus your personal Savior, you've missed what being alive is all about. God loved you so much that he sent his only Son to die for you. God loves you so much that every day he sends his Holy Spirit to talk to you and convict you of sin. God did everything he could do to throw open the pathway that leads to heaven when he resurrected his Son, Jesus, from the dead. But he cannot make the decision for you to give him your heart and life. Only you can make that decision. When you decide to ask Jesus to be your Savior and the Lord of your life, it will be the best decision you will ever make. It is the most important decision you will ever make. Believing in Jesus as your Savior will change the way you live every day of your life and it will assure that you will live in heaven forever. Please decide to make Jesus your Savior today if you have not already done so. Just pray this prayer:

Dear Jesus, I know I am a sinner. I know that my heart is far away from you. I know, too, that you are God's son and you came to die for my sins. You died to cleanse me from evil. Please come into my heart and make me clean and new. Put me on the path that leads right to heaven where you are waiting for me. Amen.

By praying this prayer and believing it in your heart, you have become a Christian, a new believer, one of God's children.

"If we confess our sins, he is faithful and just and will forgive us our sins and purify us from all unrighteousness. If we claim we have not sinned, we make him out to be a liar and his word has no place in our lives" (1 John 1:9-10).

Q: What will you tell people who don't believe that Jesus is alive?

A: So now you believe Jesus died to save you from your sins. You have confessed your sin to him and have believed he is able to wash you clean as newly fallen snow. You have asked him into your heart to be your Lord and Savior. What's next?

Remember what the disciples did when they finally realized they were forgiven, new men in Christ? They started telling everyone about how God loved them and that they needed to make their hearts right with God by confessing their sin, believing Jesus was the resurrected Christ who died and rose again to save them, and asking Jesus to be their Lord. Some of the people who heard this message were overwhelmed with guilt and immediately confessed their sin. Others did not.

People who never hear this good news about Jesus cannot believe in him. They cannot become believers unless someone tells them Jesus loves them. So what are you going to tell your friends about the love of Jesus that sent him to the cross to die?

A Final Word from Josh and Sean

First, ask those who are interested in learning about the resurrection if they believe that Jesus is alive. If they don't believe he is, ask why they don't believe. Do they have good reason for disbelief? Our experience is that many people choose not to believe that Jesus is alive, but they don't have good reasons for their beliefs. They've never learned about the evidence we've seen in this book. They know nothing about it, and so they either don't know what to believe, or they've decided not to believe. But if they are open to listening, you will be able to share with them why you believe that Jesus is a real historical figure who lived, was crucified, died, was buried in a tomb and three days later was resurrected from the dead.

"Make every effort to add to your faith goodness; and to goodness, knowledge; and

to knowledge, self-control; and to self-control, perseverance; and to perseverance, godliness; and to godliness, brotherly kindness; and to brotherly kindness, love. For if you possess these qualities in increasing measure, they will keep you from being ineffective and unproductive in your knowledge of our Lord Jesus Christ" (2 Peter 1:5-8).

ALSO AVAILABLE FROM JOSH McDOWELL AND SEAN McDOWELL

Available at Bookstores Everywhere!

Visit **www.regalbooks.com** to join **Regal's FREE e-newsletter.** You'll get useful **excerpts from our newest releases** and **special access to online chats with your favorite authors.** Sign up today!

www.regalbooks.com

BACK COVER MATERIAL

JESUS DIED ON THE CROSS, BUT THAT WASN'T THE END OF THE STORY!

Jesus' followers believed that he was the person God promised to send who would free them from the Romans, the cruel invaders who had taken over their land. So when the Romans sentenced Jesus to die on a cross, his followers' hopes were crushed. How could Jesus free them if he was dead? But his death wasn't the end of the story...

Because people don't normally come back to life, it might be tempting to believe that it has never happened. But now you can see the proof for yourself! Find out why hundreds of millions of Christians since the time of Jesus have been convinced that he died and then rose again. And find out how this truth can completely transform your life forever.

***

Since beginning his ministry in 1961, JOSH McDOWEL has given more than 23,000 talks to over 10 million young people in 115 countries. His books have sold more than 51 million copies worldwide. These include *More Than a Carpenter* and *Children Demand a Verdict,* the popular children's edition of his bestselling *Evidence That Demands a Verdict.*

SEAN McDOWELL heads the Bible department at Capistrano Valley Christian Schools. He coauthored *Understanding Intelligent Design* and *Ethix: Being Bold in a Whatever World,* and is the general editor of *The Apologetics Study Bible for Students.* Sean is a nationally recognized speaker (www.seanmcdowell.org).

Books For ALL Kinds of Readers

At ReadHowYouWant we understand that one size does not fit all types of readers. Our innovative, patent pending technology allows us to design new formats to make reading easier and more enjoyable for you. This helps improve your speed of reading and your comprehension. Our EasyRead printed books have been optimized to improve word recognition, ease eye tracking by adjusting word and line spacing as well as minimizing hyphenation. Our EasyRead SuperLarge editions have been developed to make reading easier and more accessible for vision-impaired readers. We offer Braille and DAISY formats of our books and all popular E-Book formats.

We are continually introducing new formats based upon research and reader preferences. Visit our web-site to see all of our formats and learn how you can Personalize our books for yourself or as gifts. Sign up to Become A RHYW Registered Reader.

www.readhowyouwant.com

CPSIA information can be obtained
at www.ICGtesting.com
Printed in the USA
BVHW012219220321
603236BV00014B/268